SKETCHES OF THE FRENCH REVOLUTION: A SHORT HISTORY OF THE FRENCH REVOLUTION FOR SOCIALISTS
BY
E. Belfort Bax

SKETCHES OF THE FRENCH REVOLUTION: A SHORT HISTORY OF THE FRENCH REVOLUTION FOR SOCIALISTS

Published by Etienne Publishing Group

New York City, NY

First published 1890

Copyright © Etienne Publishing Group, 2015

All rights reserved

ABOUT ETIENNE PUBLISHING GROUP

France has been the center of Western culture for centuries, and <u>**Etienne Publishing Group**</u> celebrates all aspects of French history by digitally reproducing the most important works ever written by and about Frenchmen.

Part I

The Literary Prologue

The cardinal idea of the French Revolution was the political emancipation of the middle-class. The feudal hierarchy of the Middle Ages consisted in France, as in other countries, of three main social divisions, or estates, as they were termed, (1) The superior territorial clergy, (2) the nobles, and (3) the smaller landholders, the free tenants, and the citizens of the independent townships. The mere serf, villein (holding by servile tenure), or common labourer, was like the slave of antiquity, unclassified. The possession or (non-servile) tenure of land was the condition of freedom. This third estate was the germ of our middle-class. The great problem of the French Revolution, then, was to obtain the independence and domination of the third estate. It is expressed in the words of its representative, the Abbé Sièyes "What are we of the third estate? Nothing. What would we be? Everything." But, although the political supremacy of the middle-class was the central idea, and the one which it realised (thereby effectually refuting a certain order of politicians that declares violent revolutions to be necessarily abortive), there were issues raised – and not merely raised, but carried for the time being -which went far beyond this. But the flood-tide of the Revolution did not represent the permanent gain of progress. The waters receded from the ground touched at the height of the crisis; leaving the enfranchisement of the bourgeoisie as the one achievement permanently effected.

Foremost among the precursors of this mighty change was the Genevese thinker Jean Jacques Rousseau (1712-78). This remarkable personality may aptly be termed the Messiah of the Revolutionary Crisis. His writings were quoted and read as a new gospel by wellnigh all the prominent leaders of the time. Rousseau's doctrines were contained in an early essay on civilisation, in his Emile, a treatise on Education, and in the Contrat Social, his chief work.

In his first essay, Rousseau maintained the superiority of the savage over the civilised, state, and the whole of his subsequent teaching centred in deprecation of the hollowness and artificiality of society, and in an inculcation of the imperative need of a return, as far as might be, to a state of nature in all our relations. This he especially applies to education in his Emile, in which he sketches the training of a hypothetical child.

The Social Contract, his, greatest work contains a discussion of the first principles of social and political order. It is to this work the magic formulas which served as watchwords during the Revolution, formulas such as "Liberty, Equality, and Fraternity," "Divine Right of Insurrection," the term "Citizen," employed as a style of address, and many other things are traceable. The title of the work was suggested by Locke's (or perhaps Hobbes') supposition of a primitive contract having been entered into between governor and governed. This idea Rousseau denies, in so far as any unconditionally binding agreement is concerned. No original distinction existed between, rulers and ruled. 'Any contract of the kind that obtained was merely a political convenience strictly subject to conditions. Governors were merely the delegates or mandatories of the people.

The form of government was to Rousseau more or less a minor matter, though a democracy had the most advantages, Yet it was quite possible for the mandates of the people to be adequately carried out by a special body of men (an aristocracy), or even by one man (a king. But every form of government was bound to recognize the will of the people as sovereign in all things.

The classification of the French Revolution is also largely traceable to Rousseau. The Roman constitution is invariably the source of his illustrations and the model to be copied or amended.. As regards toleration, Rousseau would allow the civil power the .right of suppressing views which were deemed contrary to good citizenship Like the Romans, he would tolerate all religions equally that did not menace the State. There is probably no single book that has produced such stupendous results within a few years, if at all, as Rousseau's Social Contract. It is the text-book of the French Revolution. Every ordinance, every law, every draft of constitution bears the mark of its influence. Although unquestionably right in his repudiation of Locke's crude theory, it is needless to say that Rousseau's own views are singularly barren and unhistorical as every theory must be that deals only with the political side of things. One may admire his loathing at the artificiality of the world around him; at the "organised hypocrisy" called religion and morality; but in his day it was impossible to uncover its historical roots, and hence, to modern ears, his diatribes lose much of their effect.

The influence of the second important precursor of the French Revolution, Francois-Marie Arouet de Voltaire (1694-1778) was much more. indirect than that of Rousseau. Voltaire's influence was almost purely negative. By his wit he scorched the reverence remaining in the minds of men for the forms of the old outworn feudal-Catholic organisation. Though there was a great amount of adroit self-seeking in Voltaire's character, it is as impossible to deny that there was much that was genuine and truly noble in his indignation at cruelty, an his detestation of Christian hypocrisy, as that it produced a far-reaching effect on the events that followed. Voltaire, although personally a Frenchman of Frenchmen, breathes the spirit of conscious cosmopolitan and contempt for nationality in his writings in which for the first time in history became a popular creed during the Revolution, and was expressed in the famous appeal of 1793.

But in this, as in other respects, Voltaire was not alone. He partly created and partly reflected the prevalent tone of the French salon (drawing-room) culture of the eighteenth century. This, if we cared to do so, we might trace back in its main features to the revival of learning – to the courts of the Medicis. And here it may be well to remind our readers, in passing, of the truth that individual genius merely means the special faculty of expressing the "spirit of the age" to which that of preceding ages has led up and that Voltaire and Rousseau merely achieved the results they did by reason of their capacity for reproducing in words the shapeless thoughts of millions. To this, in the case of Voltaire, must be added a special width of intellectual sympathy which took in an unusually large number of different subjects.

Besides Rousseau and Voltaire, we must not omit to mention the brilliant group of contemporary workers and thinkers, headed by Diderot and D'Alembert, who built up that monument of laborious industry, the great French Encyclopaedia. Immense difficulties attended the publication of this important work, notwithstanding that care was taken to exclude any expressions of overt contempt or hostility towards current prejudices. Again, we must not forget the Materialist-Atheists, central among whom was Baron Holbach, the anonymous author of the celebrated System of Nature, a book which, though crude according to modern notions, did good work in its day – work, which a treatise of more intrinsic philosophical value probably would not have achieved. It is noteworthy that most of the other prominent names among the pre-revolutionary writers, including Rousseau and Voltaire, are those of ardent deists.

All these men contributed their share in preparing the mental foundation for the great upheaval which followed. It is strange, however, that not one of them lived to see the practical issue of their labours. Rousseau, the most directly powerful of them died eleven years before the taking of the Bastille, and Voltaire the same year. Diderot lived till 1784; D'Alembert died the previous year. Mirabeau, alone of all who had prepared the great crisis, lived to see its beginning. But even he succumbed in 1791, a year and a-half before the actual fall of the monarchy. These men saw only a free thinking, aristocracy and literary class. Of the movement below they recked little, scarcely, perhaps that there was such a movement. The throne seemed secure; religion as popular as ever, the same throne which in a few years was destined to be involved in so mighty an overthrow.

Ten years of bad harvests aggravated by an effete industrial, fiscal, and political system, culminated with the summer of 1788. A great drought was succeeded by a violent hailstorm, which dealt destruction all round. The harvest was worse than ever before. All kinds of agricultural crops failed miserably all over France, not alone wheat and grain generally, but vines, chestnuts, olives; in short; all the natural products of consumption and exportation. Even what was gathered in was so spoiled as to be almost unfit for use. From every province of France came the monotonous tale of ruin, famine, starvation. Even the comparatively well-to-do peasant-farmer could obtain nothing but barley bread of a bad quality, and water, while the less well-off had to put up with bread made from dried hay or moistened chaff, which we are told "caused the death of many children." The Englishman, Arthur Young, who was travelling through France this year, wherever he went heard nothing but the story of the distress of the people and the dearness of bread. "Such bread as is to be obtained tastes of mould, and often produces dysentery and other diseases. The larger towns present the same condition, as though they had undergone the extremities of a long siege, in some places the whole store of corn and barley has the stench of putrefaction, and is full of maggots." To add to the horrors of the situation, upon the hot and dry summer follows a winter of unparalled severity. The new year of 1789 opens with the Seine frozen over from Paris to Havre. No such weather had been experienced since 1709. As the spring advances the misery increases. The industrial crisis becomes acute in the towns, thousands of workmen are thrown out of employment. The riots and local disturbances which had for many years past been taking place sporadically in various districts, now became daily more frequent, so much so that from March onwards the whole peasantry of France may be said to have been in a state of open insurrection, three hundred separate risings is the provinces being counted for the four months preceding the taking of the Bastille.

The Economic Prelude in the Provinces

In 1787, the minister Lomerie de Brienne had created nineteen new provincial assemblies. Below the arrondissement, or district assembly, which had been instituted some years before now, came the assembly of the parish. In each of these primary assemblies of the parish; the arrondissement, and even of the province, the "people, farmers, &c., sat side by side with the local dignitaries," a fact which, as may be imagined, considerably tended to obliterate the ancient feudal awe. In November, 1787, the King announced his intention of convoking the States General. On the 5th of July, 1788, the various local bodies we're called upon to draw up cahiers, or statements of their grievances for presentment before the King and States General, in which a double representation of the "third estate," was conceded. These cahiers form a mass of the most interesting material illustrative of the condition of France just before the revolution, and have not even yet been fully investigated. "The King," said the proclamation, " desires that from the extremities of his kingdom and the least known of its habitations each may feel assurance in bringing before him his views and grievances," and this and other similar expressions were interpreted by the peasantry in the natural sense that the King was really desirous of rescuing them from starvation. It accordingly emboldened them to take the matter into their own hands. In January the cahiers were drawn up, which meant that the people had now for the first time formulated their ills. Discussion in the assemblies had excited them. The States-General was going to look to their ills, it was true, but the States-General did not meet till May, and meanwhile they were starving. One thing was clear, they must have bread. Accordingly, in defiance of local authorities and guardians of the peace, bands ranging up to three or four hundred and more, formed themselves all over France, seized and plundered granaries, religious houses, stares of all kinds, entered public buildings is the name of the people, destroying all legal documents, justly regarded as the instruments of their servitude, which they could lay hands on proclaimed the local dues and taxes abolished, summarily put to death all those who interfered with them in the name of law and order, and emboldened by success, finally took to the burning of the chateaux and the indiscriminate destruction and appropriation of the houses and property of the wealthy. That the numbers of these bands were augmented not only by the workmen out of employment in Paris, Rouen, &c., but also by professional thieves, &c., was only to be expected. The local authorities were hopelessly inadequate to cope with the insurgents, the central authority in Paris seemed paralysed.

Ordinary readers of the history of the Revolution are apt to forget in following the course of events in the metropolis that they were only an enlarged picture of what was going on in hundreds of towns and villages throughout the provinces. Both before and after the famous 14th of July, in most of the provinces of France all constituted authority was at an end. No one durst disobey the mandates of the popular insurgents. It would be impossible, and tedious if it were possible, to enumerate all the circumstances of even the principal revolts. The manner was pretty much the same in all, and the following account of an insurrection at Strasburg may serve to illustrate it. Five or six hundred peasants, artisans, unemployed, tramps, and others, seize the occasion of a public holiday to attack the Hotel de Ville, the assembled magistrates escaping precipitately by back doors. The windows disappear under a volley of stones, the doors are broken in with crowbars, and the crowd enters like a torrent. "Immediately," the account states, "there was a rain of shutters, window-sashes, chains, tables, sofas, books, papers, &c." The public archives are thrown to the winds, the neigbouring streets being covered with them. Deeds Charters, &c., perish in the flames. In the cellars tuns containing valuable wines are forced, the marauders, after drinking their fill, allowing them to run until there is a pond formed five feet deep, in which several people are drowned. Others, loaded with booty, run off with it under the eyes of the soldiers, who rather encourage the proceedings than otherwise. For three whole days the city is given over to the mob. All the houses belonging to persons of local distinction are sacked from cellar to attic. The revolt spreads instantly throughout the neighbouring country, (Taine, Origines, tom i. pp.81-82).

In some districts the leaders pretended to be acting under the orders of the King. The result is everywhere at least one thing, the enforcement of a law of maximum in the price of bread, and the abolition of taxes. Atrocities, of course, occur here and there. A lawyer is half-roasted to make him surrender a charter supposed to be in his possession; a lard is tortured to death; an ecclesiastic torn in pieces. Thus have threatened ruin and starvation, to which the political and financial necessities of the King have been the occasion of giving anti Mate expression, and the remedy for which is offered to those who can read, in he Social Contract of Rousseau, become the immediate cause of the French Revolution. Although the main thread of revolutionary history is to be sought in Paris, and consequently the reader's attention in the course of the following articles will be largely occupied with the great political drama unfolding in Paris, it must never be forgotten that the life of the Revolution is simultaneously manifesting itself-that accessory dramas to that in Paris are being enacted in every town and village throughout France.

The Opening of Paris

On the 5th of May, 1789, the royal town of Versailles was gay – gay with decorations with music vocal and instrumental, with epaulettes, "etiquettes," fair women and fair costumes. It was the opening of the States General, called together for the first time since 1614, as a last resource to rescue the realm from impending bankruptcy – the opening also of the French Revolution.

At midday might have been seen the feudal procession entering the Church of St. Louis. After the King and Royal Family, the clergy occupied the first place, the "superior clergy" attired in purple robe and lawn sleeves, the less "superior" in cassock, cloak and square bonnet. Next came the nobles, habited to black with silver-faced vest, lace cravat, and plumed hat; while bringing up the rear followed the humble tiers-etat – the representatives of the middle-class, the merchants, the farmers, and the small landowners – dressed also in black, but adorned with merely a short cloak and plain hat. With this memorable procession the constitution of the middle ages, moribund for over two centuries, spasmodically gasped its last breath.

The business of the States-General did not pass off as gaily as the opening. Conflict between the orders followed immediately, with the result that the third estate constituted itself the National Assembly of France, refusing to admit the other orders to its deliberations except on a basis of equality. The King manifested his displeasure closing the door of the Hall of the States against them. The assembly answered by the celebrated oath in the tennis court of Versailles, by which it pledged itself not to separate till it had given France a constitution. The assembly triumphed over the court two days after its oath, inasmuch as it regained possession of its Hall, openly defied the King in person, got rid of the body of the clergy and noblesse, formally confirmed its decrees of the previous day which the King had quashed, and proceeded with its deliberations. Thus the curtain rose on the first act of the revolutionary drama:

Meanwhile the popular ferment had taken complete possession of the capital and was rapidly spreading into the provinces. On the 12th of July, Necker, the minister of finance, beloved by the middle-class, was dismissed from office. Necker it should be observed was one of the less bad of the scoundrels called finance ministers, who had been malversating the national funds, in succession, for years past. By comparison he appeared almost virtuous and the "populace" whose charity and admiration is always boundless toward official personages, when not quite so bad as one would expect, had converted him into an object of adoration. The city was soon in an uproar. The Palais-Royal, the great place of public assembly and political discussion, was packed with over ten thousand persons. On the table which served for a tribune, stood a young man, of fine cut features, and gentle mien who was haranguing the crowd. "Citizens," said he, "there is not a moment to lose! The removal of Meeker is the tocsin for a St. Bartholemew of patriots! This evening all the Swiss and German battalions are coming from the Champ de Mars to slaughter us! There remains but one resource let us rush to arms?" So saying, he placed in his hat a sprig of a tree – green being the emblem of hope. His example was followed till the chesnut trees of Paris were denuded.

The crowd proceeded through the streets, bearing in triumph the busts of Necker and Phillippe Egalité, its numerical strength increasing with every yard traversed, till its course was arrested on the Pont-Royal by a detachment of the Royal German Cavalry. The latter were driven back by showers of stones and the concourse swept onwards as far as the Place Louis XV. Here a formidable street fight took place, the people being opposed by a squadron of dragoons. The regulars of the King after encountering a vigorous resistance at length routed the insurgent Parisians, but the victory was more fatal to the cause they represented than any defeat could have been. The dispersed multitude carried the indignant cry, "To arms," from end to end of Paris. The regiment of the French Guards quartered in Paris mutinied and put to flight the mercenary foreign troops intended to overawe them.

The whole night long the tocsin rang out from the Hotel de Ville, where a committee of prominent citizens was sitting to organise a search for arms. The morning of the 13th July saw Paris in full revolt; the tocsins of all the churches were pealing; drums were beating along all the main streets; excited crowds collecting in every open space, gunsmith's shops being ransacked; on all sides a mad search for weapons was the order of the day. The committee at the Hotel de Ville in response to importunate demands for arms could only reply that they had none. The civic authorities next appealed to, temporised and evasively promised assistance. In the confusion there were naturally not wanting ruffians who sought to make use of the state of things prevailing for purposes of plunder. Such excesses were peremptorily put down with the cry of "death to the thieves." The equipages and other property of the "aristocrats" when seized by the people were always either destroyed or carried to a central station at the Place de Greve. In the afternoon the "provost of the merchants" (a dignitary of the effete medieval hierarchy) announced the speedy arrival of the muskets and ammunition so eagerly clamoured for on all sides. A citizen militia was formed, under the name of the Parisian Guard, numbering 48,000 men; cockades of red, blue and green were everywhere distributed; but the hours passed on and no muskets arrived. A panic seized the city that the mercenary troops were about to march on Paris during the ensuing night. At last chests purporting to contain ammunition did appear, were eagerly torn open and found to contain – old linen and broken pieces of wood.

The committee men and the "provost of the merchants" alike narrowly escaped with their lives. But the provost, pleading that he had been himself deceived, tried to divert the attention of the people by sending them on a futile expedition to Chartreux. The committee finally hit upon the device of arming the citizens with pikes, in default of firearms, and accordingly ordered 50,000 to be forged. As a measure of protection against thieves and plunderers, the city was illuminated throughout the night.

E. Belfort Bax.

P.S. Typographers have made me responsible in my last article for a couple of errors in dates, the correction of which I subjoin: – Voltaire died in 1778 – not 1718; Mirabeau died in the spring of 1791 – not 1790.

The Bastille

Next morning (the 14th) early, the word was passed among the populace "to the Invalides." There at least arms must be forthcoming. And surely enough the people were rewarded for their courage in braving the troops assembled on the Champ de Mars, and forcing their way into the great military depôt. Twenty-eight thousand muskets besides cannon, sabres and spears were carried off in triumph. Meanwhile the alarm had been given that the royal regiments posted at St. Denis were on the way to the capital and above all that the cannon of the Bastille itself was pointed toward the Boulevard St. Antoine.

The attention of Paris was at once directed to the latter point, which really commanded the most populous districts of the city. The whole morning, there was but one cry, "To the Bastille!" Armed crowds assembled at this place from all quarters, till the great fortress seemed confronted by the whole city in arms. Negotiations took place with the governor, Delaunay, but the people persistently shouted "We want the Bastille!" The die was cast by the destruction of the great bridge, which was battered down by blows from hatchets, it is said, by two men only. The concourse poured in; the second drawbridge was attacked and vigorously defended by the small garrison. Numbers of the assailants fell killed and wounded. The siege continued over four hours, when the French Guard who, as we have seen, had already sided with the revolution, arrived with cannon. The garrison, seeing the case hopeless, themselves urged the governor to surrender. But old Delaunay preferred blowing the place up and burying himself amidst the ruins. His companions alone prevented him carrying out this design. The soldiers thereupon surrendered on condition that their lives should be spared. The leaders of the people who were in the forefront and had given their word to this effect, did their utmost to protect the garrison from the indignation of the crowd. But among the thousands that thronged in there were probably few who knew, anything of what had taken place. As a consequence, Delaunay and some of the Swiss garrison fell victims to the popular fury.

Meanwhile the Hôtel de Ville was in trepidation. Above all the "provost of the merchants," Flesselles, trembled lest he should be made to suffer for his treachery. These fears were not allayed when shouts of "Victory," "Liberty," issuing from thousands of throats, assailed the ears of the inmates, and grew louder minute by minute. It was the conquerors of the Bastille carrying their heroes in triumph to the municipal head quarters. Presently there entered the great hall, an enthusiastic but disorderly, ragged, and bloodstained crowd, promiscuously armed with pikes, muskets, hatchets, and well-nigh every other conceivable weapon. Above the heads of the crowd one held up the keys of the Bastille, another the "orders" of Delaunay, a third the collar of the governor. A general amnesty for all the prisoners captured was agreed to after much opposition. But the "provost of the merchants" did not get off so easily. On the corpse of Delaunay a letter had been found, in which Flesselles had stated that he was amusing the Parisians with cockades and promises, and that if the fortress could only hold out till nightfall relief should come. A court was to have been improvised in the Palais Royal to judge him, but on the way thither he was laid dead by a pistol shot from one of the crowd.

The excitement of the day's action over, the fears of designs against the capital on the part of the Court redoubled. Everywhere barricades were raised, paving-stones torn up, pikes forged. The whole population was all night long at work in the streets. How well-grounded were the fears of the Parisians would have been evident to anyone behind the scenes at Versailles, where Breteuil, the prince minister, had just promised the king to restore the royal authority in three days this very right having been fixed for the expedition; and wine and presents distributed among the army in anticipation.

The assembly, which was sitting en permanence, was about to send one more deputation to the king (it had already sent two) when he appeared in person in its midst. On being informed of the events that had taken place by the "grand master of the wardrobe," he exclaimed "It is a revolt." "No, Sire!" replied the "grand master," "it is a revolution." On the king's subsequent protestations of affection for his subjects, and his statement that he had just given orders for the withdrawal of the foreign troops front Paris and Versailles, that he confided his person to the representatives of the nation alone &c., the assembly gave way to transports of joy, rose en masse and escorted him to the palace. The news spread rapidly. A revulsion of feeling took place all round, from terror to elation, from hatred to gratitude. The general jubilation was increased by the restoration of Necker, the entry of Louis XVI into Paris, and his acceptance of the tricolour cockade. Thus ended the preparatory period of the Revolution. It is needless to say the moral effect of the popular victory throughout France was immense, every town becoming henceforth a revolutionary centre.

There are one or two useful hints to be learned from this old and aft-repeated story of the fall of the Bastille. The first is of the eminent utility of popular "force" if only employed at the right moment. Beforehand it would have seemed preposterous that an "undisciplined mob" could take a fortress and paralyse the efforts of a reaction possessed of a trained army. Yet so it was.

Another point to note is the untrustworthiness of men who belong to the class which makes the revolution, and who even profess to represent it, when their personal interest and position are bound up with the maintenance of the existing order. Flesselles, a man of the third estate, its leading dignitary in the city of Paris, was yet the man who was least anxious to see the feudal hierarchy overthrown. And why? Because he played a part in it. The "third estate" had been incorporated into the medieval system. He was its representative as one of the feudal orders. Its position was subordinate indeed, but, now that it was growing in importance its leading men had much more to gain by clinging to the skirts of the noblesse, and aiding them in frustrating that complete revolution which the rank and file of the class were seeking, than in assisting the accomplishment of this revolution, which could only mean the effacement of their own personal positron. History repeats itself. Trades' Unions have won for themselves recognition and patronage in the middle-class world of to-day. Their leaders, in a similar way, do not exhibit any special desire for a change, which, though it would mean the liberation and triumph of the class they represent, would at the same time render Trades' Unions a thing of the past, no less than the Lord Mayors and Cabinet Ministers who stroke the backs of the parliamentary elect of Trades' Unions. No, verily, this is not a nice prospect – for the Trades' Union leaders.

The Constitution-Mongers

The constitution was now in full train. The Revolution up to the latter point was officially recognised. There was no harking back for any one. The first stratum of revolutionists was to the fore. Mirabeau, Lafayette and Bailly, are the central figures of the "Constituent Assembly," as this first legislature was termed; Duport, Barnave, and Lameth, its extreme men. The Comte de Mirabeau (1749-1791) one of the pre-revolutionary writers was the leader of the "moderate" party in the Assembly. His stupendous powers of oratory made him a useful ally and a dangerous, foe. This the court was not slow in discovering, and accordingly Mirabeau was soon won over by bribes to do his best to frustrate every popular measure in the assembly, while all the time professing devotion to the cause of liberty and the people. When this failed, the popular (?) orator did not disdain to resort to actual plotting.

The Marquis de Lafayette (1757-1834), of American Independence notoriety, was another member of the noblesse, who had adopted previously to the Revolution the quasi-advanced views then fashionable with his class, was the military representative of the "moderate" party, in his capacity of commandant of the National Guard, besides the henchman of Mirabeau in the assembly. Bailly (1736-1793), who was elected Mayor or Paris the day after the taking of the Bastille, coadjutated in the work of moderating the Revolution alike in his official capacity and in the Assembly. As to the "extreme men," they really represented but the most moderate form of constitutional monarchy. The situation of parties may be estimated by the fact that Barnave advocated a suspensory veto on the part of the King, while Mirabeau strenuously supported the absolute veto. And be it remembered at such a time, the right of vetoing obnoxious measures, would have been no mere matter of form. It appears, then, that even the most advanced Parliamentarians of the day were not prepared to go beyond the present Prussian constitution. Nevertheless, circumstances early forced upon this timid and comparatively reactionary assembly, some drastic political measures, such for instance as the abolition of all seignorial rights and privileges.

Its first important performance after the fall of the Bastille was the declaration of the Rights of Man, in imitation of the Americans after the successful termination of the War of Independence. The question which arose immediately subsequent to this, on the constitution of the chamber and its relations to the King, need not detain us. It is sufficient to state that while the assembly was amusing itself discussing "suspensory veto" or "absolute veto," the court, viz. Queen and Company at Versailles, were meditating the transference of the King to Metz, where the mercenary German troops were stationed and whence communication with the French noblesse who had emigrated and the reactionary foreign powers was easy, the idea being to declare Paris and the assembly rebels and march upon the capital with the view of restoring the absolute monarchy. These machinations at Versailles are interesting as having given the direction to the first great demonstration of the Proletariat during the Revolution. I say the direction, as the ultimate cause was the advice Marat had given some days before in the Ami du Peuple, when discussing the scarcity of bread.

The revolt broke out in this way. A woman beating a drum patrolled the streets crying bread! bread! She was soon surrounded by large numbers of women, who repaired to the Hotel de Ville demanding bread and arms, at the same time raising the cry "to Versailles" which was taken up by the populace generally, with the suddenness characteristic of Parisian outbreaks. The National Guard, and the French Guard eventually joined in, with such persistence and unanimity, that Lafayette after some hours of expostulation was compelled to place himself at their head, the troops having begun to march without him.

The unexpected appearance of a concourse headed by women and backed by a large armed force naturally threw the queen and court into a state of "amazement and admiration" (in the Shakespearean sense). The "household troops" at once surrounded the palace. The women however expressed peaceable intentions, and through their spokeswoman laid their grievances before the King and Assembly, describing the direness of the famine prevailing Meanwhile in the courtyard of the palace which was filled with a motley crowd a quarrel arose, an officer of the King's troop having struck a National Guard. This was the signal for immediate conflict between the two armed bodies. The people and the Nationals were furious and the collision must have resulted in bloodshed had it not been for the darkness of the night which was coming on and the prudent order given the Royal soldiers to cease from firing and to retreat.

The disturbance was eventually quelled, the crowds melting away gradually, as the night advanced. The royal family retired to rest at two o'clock; Lafayette who had remained up all night, in vain endeavoured to snatch repose for an hour or two at five a.m. Before six some members of the previous evening's crowd who had remained at Versailles, insulted one of the bodyguard, who drew upon them wounding one of their number. The sleepless "hero of two worlds" was soon upon the scene; he found considerable remnants of yesterday's gathering furiously forcing their way into the palace. The assailants were temporarily dispersed, but soon reassembled clamouring for the king. The king eventually appeared upon the balcony promising, in reply to the popular demands, that he would go to Paris with his family. The queen, the head and front of all the recent offending, next stepped on to the balcony in the company of the arch-courtier, Lafayette, who with a profound obeisance kissed the hand of the woman who had been plotting the massacre of that very "People" for whom this hypocritical charlatan had been all along professing zeal and devotion. But the humiliation of the Parisians was not even yet ended. Lafayette retiring, reappeared with one of the obnoxious bodyguard, and placing the tricolour cockade upon his breast, embraced him. At each of these "points" the assembled crowd duly cheered. The royal family then set out for Paris, and the Tuilieries became henceforth their permanent residence.

King and People or The New Constitution

After the pacific evolution of parties and events we have lately described, which occurred on the 5th and 6th of October, 1789, the course of the revolution was, for some considerable time, peaceful and parliamentary. The Assembly soon followed the Court to Paris. Its migration seemed the signal for a vigorous application of the pickaxe to the old feudal system. The chief bulwark attacked was the property and independent organisation of the Church. Prior to this, however, the Assembly had reconstituted the map of France, by abolishing the old division into Provinces, substituting for it the present one into Departments. The provinces had formed de facto independent states. The division into Departments placed the whole realm under one central administration and included the entire reorganisation of the judicial system. There were eighty-three Departments formed, which were divided into districts and these into cantons. The department had its administrative council and executive directory, as had also the district; the canton was merely an electoral subdivision. The commune or township was confided to a general council and a municipality, which were, however, subordinated to the departmental council. The whole elaborate and complex scheme seemed carefully arranged to exclude, as far as possible, the working classes and peasantry from any voice in legislation.

The nationalisation of the church lands and property generally was precipitated by the old trouble; the exhausted state of the treasury. Necker had devised every conceivable plan for raising the wind, and failed, when the last-named project was suggested as a means of at least temporarily satisfying the exigencies of the situation. It would be tiresome to describe in detail the stages by which the Assembly arrived at the final result. It is sufficient to say that the decree expropriating the church was carried on the 2nd December, and that from henceforth the churchmen as a body became the determined enemies of the new regime. At first the clergy seemed more inclined than the noblesse to compromise matters in the hope of retaining their wealth, but now that the die was cast they were implacable. The difficulties attending the sale of the ecclesiastical property, however, were too great to admit of its realisation in time for the pressing needs of the exchequer; hence the issue of assignats, or notes having a forced currency, in short the adoption of a system of paper money.

All these measures were very interesting and shoved a laudable activity on the part of the body politic, but they did not affect the crowds to be seen daily at the bakers' shops, ever and anon breaking out into tumult. The working-classes of Paris had gone to Versailles demanding simply bread, and Lafayette had given them the royal family. Any further grumbling was obviously to be suppressed with drastic measures. Accordingly martial law was proclaimed, and the municipality empowered to forcibly disperse any assembly of people after having once summoned them to retire. Lafayette was there to put this regulation into effect at the first opportunity. But it did not come yet.

The clubs were now beginning to play a part in influencing public opinion. The principal were these of the Feuillants, the Jacobins, and the Cordeliers. The first was "ministerial," that is, it was in possession of the constitutionalists, Lafayette being its guiding star. The second, destined subsequently to become the great unofficial expression of the Revolution, counted but few adherents in the Assembly, though Barnave and Lameth were among its members, and it was occasionally patronised by several of the constitution makers, including Mirabeau himself, One cadaverous figure was always conspicuous at the Jacobins – his dress and speeches alike carefully prepared – by name Maximilian Robespierre, by profession briefless barrister, a native of Arras. The third or club of the Cordeliers, was composed of an advanced section of the Jacobins. Among its constant attendants might have been seen the stalwart yeoman Danton, and the short, thick-set, sharp-featured, journalist Marat. But neither the clubs nor their rising orators at this time exercised any but a very indirect influence on the course of events, though, they energetically debated every question as it arose.

Meanwhile in spite of occasional disturbances, panics as to the King's plotting his flight, &c. affairs moved along with comparative smoothness towards the completion of the constitution, the consummation of the middle-class political order. Preparations for celebrating the anniversary of the fall of the Bastille with due solemnity went on apace. A national confederation was to be held in the Champ de Mars on this occasion in honour of the constitution. The "advanced" members of the noblesse, not to be behindhand in "patriotism" proposed in view of the national fête the abolition of titles, amorial bearings and the feudal insignia generally. The proposition was enthusiastically carried by the Assembly. Its result was naturally to rouse the keenest indignation among the nobles outside and to lead to an organised movement of aristocratic emigration.

On the 14th of July 1790, notwithstanding bad weather, might have seen the population of streaming from all sides in holiday attire, amid a blaze of tricolour-banners, hangings, cockades, to the Champ de Mars where a gigantic altar been erected, in the centre of a vast amphitheatre. The royal Family, the Assembly and the Municipality were grouped around this altar before which the Bishop of Autun performed mass in high pontifical robes, assisted by four hundred clergy in white surplices. Lafayette first ascended the altar and in the name of the national guards, of the whole realm, took the civic oath of fidelity to "the nation, the land, and the King." This was followed by salvos of artillery and prolonged shouts of "vive la nation!" "Vive le roi!" The president of the Assembly, and all the deputies the department councils, &c., next took the same oath. But the grand item of the day's programme was reached when Louis XVI. himself rose to swear, as King of France, to maintain the constitution decreed by the Assembly. This part of the performance terminated (as usual on "grand" occasions) with the appearance of the Queen holding the dauphin up aloft to the homage and admiration of the assembled multitude, who responded in one long and continuous acclamation. Chants of thanksgiving and exultant jubilation generally, closed the day's proceedings.

Such was the inauguration of the first French constitution! But despite the new and glorious liberty crowds of hungry Parisians continued to be daily turned away from the baker's shops.

A Constitution on its Beam Ends

All State functionaries, military, civil and eccelesiastical, were now compelled to take the oath of allegiance to the new order. This led to a revolt on the part of the majority of the nobles and ecclesiastics whose indignation was already roused to boiling point by the loss respectively of their privileges and revenues. Numbers of aristocratic officers left the army and the country to join their brethren across the frontier. Others, such as Bouillé, gave in with the view of gaining over the army for the counter-revolution.

Most of the clergy refused either to take the oath of allegiance or to leave their benefices, except by force being backed up in this by the enormous majority of the Bishops with the Pope at their head. The new Constitution in subordinating the ecclesiastical to the civil power was declared to involve an encroachment on ecclesiastical privilege, the Pope refusing to consecrate bishops in place of those deposed for non-compliance, and proclaiming the creation of all ecclesiastics, nominated according to the civic forms to be null and void. The ejection of non-conforming priests continued, notwithstanding, their successors being instituted by the bishops of Autun and Lida who had accepted the constitution. The opposite party retaliated by excommunicating all who acknowledged the intruders as they termed them. Thus began civil war between the Revolution and the Church. The clergy themselves prepared the soil of the popular mind for the reception and germination of the teachings of the pre-revolutionary writers which until now had been chiefly confined to the leisured and cultivated classes, by forcing it to the logical dilemma of friendship with the revolution, and enmity with Christianity, or friendship with Christianity and enmity with the revolution.

As regards the "emigrant" aristocrats, their object was to foment the hatred of the foreign powers against the revolution and to cement a coalition to effect its forcible overthrow by the invasion of the country. For well-nigh three years these intrigues with "the foreigner" were going on with the connivance of the court, until the fall of the monarchy precipitated "war to the knife" with the powers, in the shape of the campaign known as the "revolutionary war." To understand the position of affairs it is necessary to remember that since the collapse of Feudalism as a living political order, with its quarrels between the titular King and his more or less nominally vassal barons, power had been concentrated more and more in royal hands, while nationalities had become definitely fixed. The result was that the mainly internal politics of the feudal period had from the sixteenth century onwards been giving place to external politics, in which the sovereigns of Europe, having ceased to fear the rivalry of nobles within then jurisdiction, discovered causes of quarrel with their brother sovereigns without usually in the hope of gaining territory. The French Revolution marks the opening, for the continent at least, of the modern period of the struggle of sovereigns not with their nobles or with each other, but with peoples, that is with the middle-class backed by the proletariat. This struggle began is England more than a hundred years earlier than on the continent, but practically subsided again with the revolution of 1689. In a subsequent article I shall hope to go more fully into the position of England at the time of the French Revolution.

The three principal European powers were at this time England, France and Austria. Prussia was a rising monarchy and the great Muscovite empire loomed in the background. The petty German princelets might be reckoned upon to side with the greater powers.

The death of Mirabeau, in April, 1791, having removed all hope of making a successful stroke on behalf of Royalism in the Assembly, the Court turned its attention to military plotting within increased energy. On the other hand the King felt some misgivings at being re-established exclusively by the aid of foreign bayonets, more especially as his cousin, the Comte d'Artois, was the leader in the movement, and if it were successful might possibly obtain more than his due share of influence in the resuscitated realm. These considerations led the Court to turn a favourable ear to General Bouillé, whose plan was to conquer the revolution by means of the troops already at hand in the service of the King. The army was to be moved to the frontier, the royal family were then to escape into its midst, after which war was to be declared against the Assembly, and the troops to march on the capital. This arrangement was effected up to the point of the King's flight on the 21st June, 1791, almost without a hitch. Bouillé with his army was ready and waiting for the Royal party, when poor Louis was accidentally recognised at Varennes, and brouht back a prisoner to Paris. The indignation of the populace knew no bounds. The royal cortege re-entered Paris n the midst of sullen and angry crowds. For the first time talk of a Republic was heard. Barnave and the Lameth became the leaders of the Constitutionalist party in the Assembly now that Mirabeau was dead. But it was with difficulty that the Constitutionalists could reinstate the King after hits voluntary and treacherous abdication. They were only successful in their efforts, having thrown as a sop to Cerberus the condition that if he retracted his oath to the constitution, if he should place himself at the head of an army, or permit others to do so, he should lose his inviolability and be considered and treated as an ordinary citizen.

But opinion outside the Assembly was far from satisfied. The leaders of the Jacobin club (which was now the centre of a federation of similar clubs throughout the country) among whom were confounded in one cause Brissot, Pétion, Robespierre, Danton, Marat, &c., men of the "advanced" middle-class and men of the people, combined to rouse the nation against this decree, insisting on the abdication of Louis, and denying (the competency of the Assembly. They drew up a petition in which they appealed from the Assembly to (the sovereignty of the people. This petition was taken to the Champ de Mars and laid upon "the altar of the country." Thousands came to sign it; the assemblage being dispersed by Lafayette, returned subsequently in greater numbers than before. Next time the commandant of the National Guard came accompanied by Bailly, the mayor. The red flag, the then symbol of martial law, was unfurled, the summons to disperse proclaimed, after which Lafayette gave the order to fire. A murderous charge followed, in which hundreds were killed and wounded. But notwithstanding that the

Republicans were cowed for the time being, the court-sycophant and his accomplices in the work of the Constitution were well-nigh played out, though the old farce had first to be gone, through. The King once more accepted the Constitution, and in addition to the terms of his re-instatement in possession of his functions, made a touching and heart-stirring speech to the Assembly, was received thereupon with effusive demonstrations of affection, &c., &c. The Constituent Assembly which had been made up out of the abortive "States-General" then formally proclaimed itself dissolved. In the opinion of most men it was time.

The Legislative Assembly.

The new "Legislative Assembly" as it was called to distinguish it from the first or Constituent Assembly, commenced its sittings on the 1st of October, 1791. Without, the coalition of, Europe against the Revolution was complete. England was united with Russia, Prussia and Austria, while the petty German states eagerly joined in this conspiracy to suppress the French nation. The famous treaty of Pilnitz was the expression of the determination and temper of the "powers" great and small. Within, the fabric of the constitutional monarchy was standing indeed, but as Carlyle expresses it, like an inverted pyramid, which may topple over any moment. Friction began at once between the King and Assembly on questions of reciprocal etiquette which it is unnecessary to dilate upon, but the "speech from the throne," was well received. The dominant party in this Assembly was that of the Girondists, or party of compromise, the buffer so to speak between the constitutionalists proper now in the minority, and the popular and avowedly Republican party whose leaders in the clubs, Robespierre, Danton, Marat, &c., were gaining in influence every day.

Almost the first act of the new Assembly was the issue of a decree ordering the emigrants to return on penalty of death, and confiscation of goods. This order the King peremptorily vetoed. The same fate befell another order of the Assembly, by which "refractory" priests should lose their pay and be placed under surveillance. His action in these matters in view of the imminent invasion of the foreign powers and the peasant revolt in the Vendée in favour of royalism (which was led by the clergy) were fatal to him and to the constitutionalists who supported him. The constitutional ministry fell, and a Girondin ministry was appointed in its place, with Roland, one of the principal Girondin leaders, as minister of the interior, and Dumouriez as minister of foreign affairs.

The first act of the new ministry was to take the bull by the horns and declare war with Austria, a measure popular on all sides. This, declaration of war was made on the 20th of April, 1792. Three columns proceeded to the frontier, but the projected action on the offensive was a fiasco – a panic seizing the troops on the approach of the enemy. Thenceforward the French assumed the defensive. Such was the beginning of the revolutionary war. The news of the disaster led to bitter recriminations on the part of the popular party, against the Girondins. The Girondins in their turn threw the blame on the constitutionalists, and their commanders Lafayette, Dillon, &c., while the generals themselves threw it on Dumouriez. The Jacobins openly accused they "moderate" parties of treachery and connivance with the Government. Suspicion and distrust were universal. It was now that Marat issued his memorable placards calling for the heads of traitors. Meanwhile to appease the people the ministry instituted a permanent camp of 20,000 men in the neighbourhood of Paris, in spite of the vehement opposition of the constitutionalists, and agreed to the introduction into the new national guard of promiscuously selected companies armed with pikes – the weapons which had played such a prominent part at an early stage of the Revolution. The Assembly, which declared itself sitting in permanence added to these resolutions one ordering the abolition of the King's body-guard. This last decree Louis at once refused to ratify, and on being remonstrated with by Roland, dismissed all the Girondin ministers and appointed obscure members of the constitutionalist party in their stead. At the same time he sent a secret messenger to negotiate with the coalition – for his "deliverance."

The Girondins finding themselves thus left out in the cold, joined the Jacobins who were now the advanced guard of the revolution and whose organisation was rapidly becoming a rival to the Assembly, and by this means were enabled to pose as martyrs in the cause of liberty. The only hope of the party actually in power lay in Lafayette's army Lafayette, seeing the situation, played out his last card and published a manifesto openly defying and threatening the Jacobins. The Jacobins' reply to this was the, insurrection of the 20th of June, 1792, when a concourse numbering some 8,000 people left the faubourg St. Antoine for the hall of the Assembly. The orator who represented the crowd spoke in ruenacing terms, saying that the people were ready to employ all their powers in the resistance to oppression. He proceeded to state that grave complaint was found with the conduct of the war into which the people demanded an immediate investigation, but that the heaviest grievance of all was the dismissal of the patriot ministers. The Assembly replied that the memorial of the people should be taken into consideration and ?????? while exhorted them to respect the laws. By this time the multitude numbered some 30,000 men women and children, including many national guards and with a liberal sprinkling of pikes, flags and revolutionary emblems among them this motley concourse poured into the hall singing the Ça ira, and shouting "Long live the people!" "Long live sans-culottes!" On leaving Assembly the cry was to the palace, where the crowd swept through the open gates into the apartments and corridors, and were proceeding to demolish the doors with blows when Louis himself appeared accompanied by only a few attendants. The multitude still pressing in, he took his station in the opening of a window. There he remained seated on a chair, placed on a table and protected from the pressure of the crowd by a cordon of national guards. To the cries of the people for his sanction to the decrees, he replied, – as the royalist historians assure us, with intense dignity – "This is neither the manner for it to be demanded of me, nor the moment to obtain it." The result of his refusal might have been awkward for him had he not had the presence of mind to take advantage of an incident which presented itself just at the moment. A red Phrygian cap, the symbol of the" people" and on "liberty" was prevented by one of the crowd on the point of a pike. This he took and placed on his head, an act which was greeted with tumultuous applause. At last Pétion, the Mayor arrived with several prominent Girondist deputies, and quietly dispersed the gathering.

Thus the silly Parisian populace were once again cajoled out of their demands, by a senseless piece of buffoonery. But it was the last time. The Constitutionalists were enraged at the outrage offered to the person of the King and to the "law." Lafayette left the army and suddenly appeared at the bar of the Assembly demanding the impeachment of the instigators of the movement of the

20th of July, and the suppression of the popular clubs. But the Jacobins had by this time got the upper hand, and could defy the champion of middle-class "law and order." Lafayette narrowly escaped arrest far deserting his army, and had ignominiously to slink back. The whole force of the popular sentiment was with the Girondins and the Jacobins. Events were fast hurrying to a crisis.

The 10th of August

Shortly after the event last described the Assembly felt itself compelled in face of the open connivance of the court with the enemy to solemnly declare the country in danger. All citizens capable of bearing arms were called upon to enrol themselves is the National Guard which was placed on a footing of active service.

On the 14th of July, the Bastille anniversary, Pétion was the hero of the day – Pétion or death being the popular watchword. All battalions of the National Guard showing signs of attachment to constitutionalism instantly became objects of popular resentment. The hatred between Constitutionalists and Republicans was daily growing. At length the popular party obtained the disbandment of the companies of Grenadiers and Chasseurs the main support of the official middle class in the National Guard together with the closing of the Feuillant's Club.

Events further helped on the popular party. On the 25th of July, the Duke of Brunswick published his manifesto in the name of the Emperor and King of Prussia in which he declared that the allied sovereigns had taken up arms to put an end to anarchy in France, threatening all the towns which dared to resist, with total destruction, the members of the Assembly with the rigours of martial law, etc. The active coalition which was at this time confined to Prussia, Austria, the German princedoms, and the principality of Turin had formed the plan of marching concentrically upon Paris from three different points, the Moselle, the Rhine, and the Netherlands. It was on the day of the movement of the Rhenish division from Coblentz under the command of the Duke of Brunswick that this famous manifesto was issued. The following day, July 26th a contingent of six hundred Marseillais entered Paris on their way to the camp at Soissons, a continent rendered immortal by the hymn they sang as they marched along, tine well known strains,

Allons, enfants de la Patrie

Le jour de gloire est arrivé.

having been heard for the first time is the streets of Paris on that day. The advent of the Marseillais, though it did not, as was anticipated, result in an immediate outbreak, did, nevertheless, stir Paris to its foundations. The sections, or wards into which the city was divided became daily more importunate in demanding the dethronement of the king. A petition to this effect was drawn up by the Municipality and the sections and presented to the Assembly by Pétion on the 3rd of August. The impeachment of Lafayette was next demanded on the 8th but after a warm discussion was rejected to a considerable majority. This acquittal of Lafayette now regarded by the people as the personification of treachery and reaction, destroyed the last vestige of popular confidence in the Assembly. The following day the section Quinze Vings sent to notify to the legislature that if the decree of dethronement were not voted before nightfall the tocsin should be sounded, the générale beaten and open insurrection proclaimed, a determination which was transmitted to the forty-eight sections of the city and approved with only one dissentient, The same evening the Jacobins proceeded in a body to the Faubourg St. Antoine and there organised the attack on the Tuilieries which it was decided should take place the next day.

Measures pregnant wish import for the future course of the revolution were determined at this meeting; such as, the dismissal of Pétion, the annulment of the Departmental Assembly, the replacement of the council of the Municipality by a Revolutionary Commune.

At midnight the tocsin pealed, the générale beat, the sections assembled, the newly nominated commune took possession of the Hotel de Ville. At the same time the "loyal" battalions of the National Guard were marched to the palace, which was now filled with Swiss Guards and Chevaliers du Cour, and the Assembly hastily called together. On hearing that Pétion was detained at the Tuilieries the moribund legislature at once ordered his release and restored him to his functions. But he no sooner entered the Hotel de Ville than he was placed under a guard of three hundred men by order of the new Commune. Poor Pétion! between two fires. The Commune then sent for the Commander of the National Guard, Mandat, who was at the Tuilieries with the "loyal" battalions aforesaid. Mandat, not knowing of the creation of the new Commune, incautiously obeyed the summons, but turned pale on discovering new faces when he had expected to find the old Municipality. He was accused of having authorised the troops to defend the Palace against the sovereign people, was ordered to the prison of the Abbaye but assassinated on the steps of the Hotel de Ville as he was being conveyed within. Santeen was then nominated commander-in-chief in his stead.

Meanwhile not a few "nationals" at the palace, in spite of their loyalty to the Constitution winced at finding themselves in the same gallery with aristocratic adventurers, avowed enemies of the revolution in any form or shape and with mercenary foreign soldiers. Their leader gone, a division broke out as Louis found when he came to review them, for while the cry vive le roi was responded to by some, vive la nation was responded to by more. But what was most ominous was the arrival of two fresh battalions armed with pikes as well as guns, who after jeeringly greeting the King with shouts of vive la nation, "down with the veto," "down with the traitor," took up position at the Pont Royal and pointed their cannon straight at the Palace. It was evident the loyalty of these battalions was more than a doubtful quality. The insurgents were now advancing in columns of various strength from different points. The Procurator Syndic, Roederer met them as they were converging upon the palace, and suggested their sending a deputation to the king. This was peremptorily refused. He then addressed himself to the National Guard, reading out the Articles of the law which enjoined them to suppress revolt. But the response was so feeble that the Procurator fled in all haste back to the Tuileries to urge the royal family to leave their quarters, and place itself in the midst of the Assembly, out of harm's reach. Marie-Antoinette rejected the advice in right transpontine melodramatic style, talked very "tall" about being "nailed to the halls of the palace," and presented a pistol to Louis with the words "Now; sire, is the moment to show your courage." The procurator evidently thought mock heroics ill-timed, and sternly remonstrated. Louis himself seemed to share this opinion, or at least was not prepared "to show" his "courage" just then, and moved to go to the Assembly. Marie-Antoinette followed with the royal youth, and thus what bid fair to be a dramatic "situation" came to an ignominious ending.

Meanwhile the insurgents surrounded the palace, the defence of which was left to the Swiss Guard, who though they fought with a valour worthy of a better cause, were ultimately overwhelmed by numbers and exterminated. The palace taken, shouts of victory rent the air (as epic historians would say). The Assembly trembled expecting every minute the hall to be forced. In vain it issued a proclamation conjuring the people to respect magistrates, laws, and justice, &c. At length the new Commune presented itself, claiming the recognition of its powers, the dethronement of the king, and the convocation of a national convention. Deputation after deputation followed with the same prayer, or rather the same peremptory order. The Assembly over-awed, on the motion of the Girondist Vergniaud, passed a resolution in pursuance of the demands, that is, suspending the King, dismissing the constitutionalist ministers and ordering the convocation of a national convention. The person of Louis was handed over to the Commune, by whose order he was conveyed a virtual prisoner to the Temple. Thus ended the 10th of August, 1792. The critical struggle is henceforth not, as heretofore between the middle classes and the nobles or the king, but between, the middle classes and the Proletariat.

Part II

The First Paris Commune and the September Massacres.

With the 10th of August and the virtual overthrow of the monarchy the first part of the French Revolution may be considered as ended. The middle-class insurrection proper had done its work. It would be a mistake, too, to underrate the importance of that work from certain points of view. In a word, it had abolished, not, indeed, Feudalism, in its true sense – for that had long since ceased to exist – but the corrupt remains of Feudalism, and the monarchical despotism it left behind it. The beginning of '89 found France cut up into provinces, each in many respects an independent state, possessing separate customs, separate laws, and sometimes a separate jurisdiction. The end of '89 even and still more '92, found it, for good or for evil, a united nationality. The power of to clergy and noblesse was completely broken. Judicial torture and breaking on the wheel were absolutely done away with. Madame Roland has described the dying cries of the victims of "justice," who, after having been mangled by the latter hideous engine, were left exposed on the market-place, "so long as it shall please God to prolong their lives." All this, then, was abolished, and in addition the "goods" of the clergy and of the "emigrant" nobility were declared confiscated. The interesting point as yet unsolved was, who should get this precious heritage, the "nationalised" houses and moveable possessions of the recalcitrant first and second estates? To avoid interrupting the narrative we shall devote a chapter to the elucidation of this point later on.

We come now to what we may term the great tidal wave of the revolution. For the time being it swept call before it, but it receded as quickly as it came. The period of the ascendancy, of the proletariat lasted from the 18th of August, 1792, to the 27th of July, 1794, thus in all nearly two years. The political revolution suddenly became transformed into a revolution one of whose objects at least was greater social and economical, as distinguished from political, equality, and as suddenly ceased to be so. The course of the progress and retrogression of this movement we shall trace in the following chapters.

The new revolutionary municipality, or commune of Paris, was now for the time being the most powerful executive body in all France. It dictated the action even of the Assembly. The establishment of an extraordinary tribunal bad been proposed. The Assembly hesitated to agree with it. Thereupon it received a message from the commune that if such a tribunal wire not forthwith constituted, an insurrection should be organised the following night which should overwhelm the elect of France. The Assembly yielded under the pressure, and a Court was formed which condemned a few persons, but was soon after abolished by the Commune as inadequate. At the head of the latter body were Marat, Panis, Collot d'Herbois, Billaud-Varennes, Tallien, &c. but the most prominent. man of all was for the moment, Danton, who was untiring in organising the "sections" (as the different wards of the city were called), and who, from having been the chief agent in the events of the 10th had acquired almost the position of dictator.

Meanwhile the invading army of the Prussians had crossed the frontier, while the French frontier troops at Sedan deserted by Lafayette were disorganised and without a commander. On the 24th of August, the citadel of Longwy capitulated, and by the 30th the enemy were bombarding the town of Verdun. In a few days the road to Paris would lie open before them. Consternation prevailed in the capital at the news. In a conference between the ministry and the recently formed committee of general defence, Danton boldly urged, as against a policy of waiting or of open attack, that one of terrorism should be adopted, to first intimidate the reactionary population of the city, and through them that of the whole country. "The 10th of August," said he, "has divided France into two parties. 'The latter, which it is useless to dissemble, constitutes the minority in the State, is the only one on which you can depend when it comes to the combat" The timid and irresolute Committee hesitated; Danton betook himself to the Commune. His project was accepted. The minority had indeed to fight the majority. Domiciliary visits were made during the night, and so large a number of suspected persons arrested that the prisons were filled to overflowing. All citizens fit to carry arms were enrolled on the Champ de Mars, and dispatched to the frontier on the 1st of September. About two o'clock the next day, Sunday, the great bell or tocsin was sounded, the call-drum or générale was beaten along the thoroughfares, the famous September massacres were at hand. Danton, in presenting himself before the Assembly to detail the measures that had been taken (without its consent) for the safety of the country, gave utterance to his celebrated mot – "Il faut de l'audace, de l'audace, et toujours de l'audace" (We must have boldness, boldness, and always boldness). The previous night all the gates of the City had been closed by order of the municipality, so that none could leave or enter; to the clanging of the tocsin and the roll of the générale was now added the firing of alarm cannon. Herewith began the summary executions, as they would have been called had they been done in the interests of "established order" by men in uniform, or massacres, as they have been termed since they were effected in the interests of revolution by men in bonnet rouge and Carmagnole costume. The matter originated with the destruction of thirty priests who were being conducted to the Abbaye. The prisons, about seven in number, were then visited, in succession by a band of some three hundred men. Entrance was demanded by an improvised court, who once inside, with the prison-registers open before them, began to adjudicate. The prisoners were severally called by name, their cases decided in a few minutes, after which they were successively removed nominally to another prison or to be released. No sooner, however, had they reached the outer gate than they were met by a forest of pikes and sabres. Those that were deemed innocent of treasonable practices, and were "enlarged" with the cry of "vive la nation" (Long Live the Nation) were received with embracings and acclamation, but woe betide those who were conducted to the entrance in silence. Upon them the pikes and sabres at once fell, in some cases veritably hewing them in pieces. The Princess de Lamballe, the friend and maid of honour to Marie Antoinette, had just gone to bed when the crowd arrived at the Abbaye where she was imprisoned. On being informed that she was about to be removed; she wanted; to arrange her dress, she said; at which the bystanders hinted that from the distance she would have to go it was scarcely worth while to waste much time on the toilette. Arrived at the gate, her head was struck off, and her body stripped and disembowelled. Carlyle goes into an ecstatic frenzy over this incident. "She was beautiful, she was good," he exclaims (vol. iii. chap. 4), in a style suggestive of an Irish wake, in which whisky has played a leading part. "Oh! worthy of worship, thou king-descended, god-descended," &c. He pathetically talks about her "fair hind-head," meaning to imply, I suppose, that she had a long thin neck. But inasmuch as there is no physiological reason for supposing that a long thin neck involves greater suffering in the process of decapitation than a short thick one, the point of the remark is not obvious. Be this as it may, the princesses' head, with others, was paraded on a pike through the streets and under the windows of the "temple," where the queen was confined. These summary executions or massacres (according as we choose to call them) outside the prisons continued at intervals from the Sunday afternoon to the Thursday evening. Probably about 1,200 persons in all perished. All contemporary writers agree in depicting the graphic horror of the scene as the bloodstained crowd swept along the streets from prison to prison.

There is no doubt that the principal actors in these events were either under the orders, or were at least in communication with the Commune, but the precise nature of the connection has not been, and probably now never will be known. That those concerned were no mere wanton or mercenary ruffians, but fanatics, possessed by a frenzy of despair, is amply proved by several incidents which are admitted even by Royalist writers. Their enthusiasm at the discovery of a "patriot" in one whom they believed to have been a "plotter," as in the case of M. de Sombreuil, and their refusal of money from such, their evident desire to avoid by any accident the death of an innocent person, show the executioners to have been at least genuinely disinterested. There has never in all history been more excuse for the shedding of blood than there was in Paris, at the beginning of September, 1792. Foreign troops were marching on the capital to destroy the Revolution, and all favourable to it. The city itself was honeycombed with Royalist plotters, who almost openly expressed their joy at the prospect of an approaching restoration and the extermination of the popular leaders. The so-called massacres were strictly a measure of self-defence, and as such were justified by the result; which was, in a word, to strike terror into the reaction, and to stimulate the Revolution throughout France; and yet there are bourgeois who pretend to view this strictly defensive act of a populace driven to desperation, with shuddering horror, while regarding as "necessary," or at most mildly disapproving the wanton and cold-blooded massacres of the Versailles soldiers after the Commune of 1871. Such verily is class blindness! As in all great crises in history, so in the French Revolution, an active minority had to fight and terrorise the stolid mass of reaction and indifference, which, alas is always in the majority.

The National Convention

While these events were going on in Paris, Dumouriez, the successor of Lafayette as commander-in-chief of the French army, was in the east organising the resistance to the invasion. Verdun was taken by the Prussians almost without resistance. But the new commander, who, whatever else he may have been, was a man of military genius, saw at a glance the strategical situation and, in opposition to the council of war, decided to lose no time in occupying the passes of the mountainous district of the Argonne, He circumvented the enemy by forced marches, and they soon found the road to Paris barred by precipitous rocks and well-guarded passes. The Prussians, notwithstanding, forced one of the more feebly defended of the positions, and were on the point of surrounding the French army when Dumouriez, by a dexterous retreat, succeeded in evading them till the arrival of his reinforcements. Meanwhile, the weather helped the defendants. Heavy rains converted the bad roads into rivers of mud knee deep, and it was not until the 20th of the month that the main body of the invaders reached the heights of Valmy, where General Kellerman was in command, and which they attempted to storm. The result decided the fate of the invasion. The Prussians and Austrians were completely defeated to the cry of "Vive La Nation," and retired in disorder. Up to this time the fortunes of war had been unremittingly adverse to the French. But the turning point had come. Henceforward the revolutionary army, who from this moment assumed the offensive, went forth with little intermission conquering and to conquer. The present sketch not being a history of the revolutionary war, but of the revolution itself, I shall in future only allude to the military situation in so far as it affects the course of internal affairs.

The moribund Legislative Assembly lingered on during the election of the Convention; which did not open its deliberations till then 21st of the month. After the usual preliminaries it formally abolished Royalty and proclaimed the Republic. Its next measure was to declare the new era date from the current year as the first year of the French Republic. These measures were carried by acclamation. But the Convention almost immediately became the prey of internal dissension. This most remarkable of legislative bodies embraced every shade of opinion and almost all the men of any prominence in public life. Robespierre, Danton, Marat, Desmoulins, David Roland, Barbaroux, Sièyes, Barrere; &c.; were all now to the fore with many others, such as Tallien, Collot d'Herbois, Billaud, Varennes, Barras, &, hitherto less known to fame, but shortly to come into unmistakable prominence. One feature of the Convention is especially remarkable. It embodied the first conscious recognition of the principle of Internationalism. The German atheist, internationalist, and humanitarian, Anarchis Clootz, and the English, freethinking and republican Thomas Paine were among its members. Priestley, of Birmingham, the great chemist, had also been elected, but declined to sit.

The two great parties in the Convention were the Girondists and the Mountainists. The

Girondists were the party of orderly progress, sweetness and light the men who dreaded all violent, i.e., energetic measures, in short, the Karl Pearsons of the Revolution. Such men, however well-intentioned they may be, must always in the long run become the tools of reaction from their timidity and hesitancy. The Girondists desired a doctrinaire republic, led by the professional middle-classes, the lawyers and literateurs. Their main strength lay in the provinces, the name being derived from the department of the Gironde, whence some, of their chief men came. Among the leaders of the Girondist Party may be mentioned Condorcet, Roland, Petion, Barbaroux; Vergniaud and Brissot. Some of them had been, in spite of their generally mild attitude, active in preparing the 10th of August. It was Barbaroux who sent to his native town for the Marsellais, and directed this remarkable body of men on the day of the insurrection.

The other leading party in the Convention were the Mountainists, as they were termed, because they sat on the benches at the top of the left, comprising the leaders of Paris and virtually identical in policy with Commune, many of whose members sat in both the municipal and the legislative bodies. Robespierre, Danton and Marat and all the most advanced Revolutionary leaders belonged to the "Mountain", which had its strength in the 48 "sections," and in the faubourgs, or outlying suburbs, in which the populace of Paris found voice. The Mountainists advocated uncompromising revolutionary principles (besides aiming to some extent, at economic equality) a vigorous policy and strong centralisation in, opposition to the Girondists, who favoured strictly middle-class republicanism, a timid and vacillating policy, and federalisation, or local autonomy. The struggle between the Mountain and the Gironde was in part a struggle for supremacy between Paris and the departments. Besides the Mountainists and Girondists proper – i.e., those who represented any definite principles at all, who both together constituted a minority in the Convention, notwithstanding that they decided its character and policy there was the actual majority which was called the Plain, its members being sometimes designated in ridicule, "frogs of the marsh". Like most majorities, the Plain, was an inchoate mass of floating indifferentism and muddle-headedness, with more or less reactionary instincts, which; naturally inclined it to the side of the Girondists as the "moderate" party, but whose first concern being self preservation was open to outside pressure from the armed "sections" of Paris and the faubourgs as we shall presently see. These "men of the plain" or "frogs of the marsh" included many persons of ability who subsequently came to the front under the Directorate after all danger of popular insurrection was at an end.

War was declared within the Convention, before many days were over, by the Gironde, on the ostensible pretext of the September massacres which they accused the partisans of the Mountain of having instigated. The individuals attacked were Robespierie, and Marat. It was the turn of Robespierre first, He was accused of aspiring to the dictatorship, and the whole force of Girondist eloquence was brought to bear upon the form and cadaverous ex-advocate of Arras, though without result. No definite charges could be formulated against him. It is significant nevertheless, that before Robespierre had attained any especial prominence he should have excited feelings of such keen personal animosity. As a matter of fact, Danton had had far more directly, to do with the so-called massacre than Robespierre. It was Marat's turn next. Marat, whose single-mindedness and absolute self-sacrifice are almost unique in history, had the misfortune to be physically an unattractive personality. He suffered from an unpleasant skin malady; which, as it happens, was not syphilis as many writers have hinted, but seems to have been of the nature of the sheep-disease, known as scabies. It was very possibly contracted, and without doubt considerably aggravated through the starvation and cellar-life he was compelled to lead during the early part of the Revolution. However this may be, Marat was denounced in the Convention by the Girondins, and when are arose, to defend himself he was for a moment basely deserted by even his colleagues of the Mountain. "I have a great many enemies in this Assembly," he said, as he rose to reply to his accusers. "All! All!" shouted the Convention as one man. However, Marat proceeded amidst uproar and howls to exculpate himself, till in the end the simple earnestness of his eloquence prevailed and he sat down amid a storm of applause. But the Girondists though discomfited for, the time, did not lose sight of their designs to destroy Marat. In the midst of these recriminations and internal squabbles, the Mountain succeeded in getting the unity of the Republic decreed, a heavy blow to the Federalist Girondins.

The Trial and Execution of the King

A truce to personal questions having been for a moment agreed upon the Convention was proceeding to discuss the new constitution when, op the motion of the Mountain, the question of the disposal of the King was declared urgent. The popular resentment against the dethroned monarch had been growing for some time past. Continual addresses from the departments, as well as from the Paris sections, were being received praying for his condemnation. The usual legal questions being raised as to the power of any tribunal to try the sovereign, it was agreed by the Committee appointed to consider the matter that though Louis had been inviolable as King of France, he was no longer so as the private individual Louis Capet. The Mountain vehemently attacked this view. St. Just, Robespierre, and others declared that these legal quibbles were an insult to the people's sovereignty, that the King had already been judged by virtue of the insurrection, and that nothing remained but his condemnation and execution. Just at this time an iron chest was found behind a panel of the Tuilleries, containing damning proofs of Court intrigues with Mirabeau, and with the "emigrant" aristocrats, also indicating that the war with Austria had been declared with a view to betraying the country and the Revolution. This naturally gave force to the demand for the immediate condemnation of Louis as a "traitor to the French and guilty towards humanity." The agitation was vigorously sustained in the Jacobins' club and in the sections, and the "moderate" party in the Assembly found itself compelled to give heed to the popular outcry, at least up to a certain point. The Convention by a considerable majority decided against the extreme right, who urged the inviolability of the King, and also against those Mountainists who pressed for a condemnation without trial. It was determined to bring the ex-King to the bar of the Convention. The Act declaratory of the Royal crimes was then prepared.

Meanwhile Louis was being strictly guarded in the "Temple," where he had now been confined nearly four months. He had recently been separated from his family, the Commune fearing the concerting of plots of escape, &c. Only one servant was allotted to the whole family. Louis amused himself at this time with reading Hume's History of England, especially the parts relating to Charles I. On the vote of the Convention being declared, Santerre, the commandant of the National Guard was commissioned to conduct Louis to the bar of the National Assembly. This took place on the 11th of December. The coach passed through drizzling rain, scowling crowds, and through streets filled with troops. Arrived at the Hall of the Convention, the Mayor of Paris, Chabot, and the Procureur, Chaumette, who had sat with the King in the vehicle, delivered him over to Santerre, who had been in attendance outside. The latter, laying hold of Louis by the arm, led him to the bar of the Convention. Barriere, the president, after a moment's delay, greeted him with the words, "Louis, the French nation accuses you; you are now about to hear the act of accusation. Louis, you may sit down." There were fifty-seven counts of the indictment relating to acts of despotism, conspiracies, secret intrigues, the flight to Varennes, and what not. On the conclusion of the speech for the prosecution, which lasted three hours, Louis was removed back to his prison. He had demanded legal counsel, so the Convention decided after some discussion to allow his old friend Malesherbes, with two others, Tronchetand Désezé, to undertake the office. It was the latter who delivered the speech on the day of the defence, which consisted partly in the old arguments anent royal inviolability and partly in a statement of Louis's services to the people "The people," said Désezé, desired that a disastrous impost should abolished, and Louis abolished it; the people asked for the abolition of servitudes, and Louis abolished them; they demanded reforms, and he consented to them," &c., &c. The speech concluded with an eloquent peroration calling history to judge the decision of the assembly. The cowardly Girondins, although it was well-known they had previously been in favour of the King's life, did not have the courage at this moment to make a definite stand one way or the other. They contented themselves with proposing to declare Louis guilty, but to leave the question of punishment to the primary assemblies of the people. This proposition, which would probably have meant civil war, was vehemently opposed by the Mountain and rejected, and the Convention, after having unanimously voted Louis guilty, resolved on considering the question of punishment. The popular ferment outside the Convention was immense, and sentence of death was loudly demanded. After forty hours, the final vote was taken, and Louis condemned to "death without respite," i.e., within twenty-four hours, by a majority of 26 in an assembly of 721. In vain did the defenders urge the smallness of the majority; the Mountain, which now for the first time dominated the Convention, showed itself inexorable.

On Monday, the 21st of January, 1793, the execution took place. Louis, who had taken leave of his family the previous day, was awakened at five o'clock. Shortly after, Santerre arrived to announce that it was the hour to depart. At the same time the murmur of crowds and the rumbling of cannon was heard outside. The carriage took upwards of an hour to pass through the streets lined with military. At length the Place de la Revolution was reached, and Louis ascended the scaffold. He was beginning to protest his innocence, when on the signal of Santerre his voice was drowned by the beating of drums, the executioners seized him, and in a moment all was over. The death of Louis was probably necessary for the safety of the Republic at the time, but one cannot help having a certain pity for one whose worst offences were a certain feebleness and good nature which made him the ready tool of a cruel, unscrupulous, and designing woman. It should be noted, as regards the decree in the Convention, that, unlike the Girondins, plucky Tom Paine, up to the last, manfully voted in the sense in which he had always spoken, viz., for the life of the King, and this at the imminent risk of his own. Notwithstanding this act a grateful Respectability (which afterwards tried to exalt the feeble idiot Louis into a hero and a martyr) has ever since heaped every vile calumny on poor Paine's memory.

The Death Struggle Between Mountain and Gironde

On the evening of the final vote in the Convention on the matter of the King. Lepelletier de St. Fargeaur, the deputy and ex-noble, who had voted with the majority, was assassinated by an ex-royal guard in a cafe. On the Thursday following he received a public funeral, his remains being interred in the Pantheon of great men. The Convention, Municipality, and all the revolutionary societies followed in a body. This was the last united action of the various parties.

The feud between Mountain and Gironde broke out with renewed fury after the temporary cessation. The quarrel was intensified out of doors by the old but ever-increasing lack of the necessaries of life, especially of bread. The queues at the bakers' shops assumed more formidable dimensions, developing into mobs and devastating provision shops. Marat had suggested in his journal that a few of the forestallers who were helping to keep up the price of bread should be hanged at the doors of the bakers' shops. The crowds, dressed in carmagnole, or merely sans-culotte maddened by hunger; danced the more wildly to the well-known strains, "Vive le son du canon." Day and night groups or these revolutionary revellers, might be met along the thoroughfares. Meanwhile "the sound of the cannon" was t going on with vigour and to the honour and glory of France. Dumouriez had invaded and conquered the Netherlands, and the Jacobins and other revolutionary bodies had sent missionaries to the newly-annexed provinces. But the powers, great and small, finding themselves and the aristocratic-monarchic order they represented being beaten all along the line, drew close together and made new levies. England, Spain, Italy, Austria Prussia the small German States, even Russia, hurled new and gigantic armaments into the breach. The Convention answered in its turn by a fresh levy of 300,000 men. But the Mountain demanded at the same moment that while external enemies were being fought internal enemies should not be neglected. They proposed that a tribunal composed o: nine members should judge without jury and without appeal. The tribunal was instituted but the jury added. Dumouriez now sustained some reverses in his invasion of Holland. He was ordered back into Belgium, but this did not satisfy the Mountain and the Jacobins, who had for long looked askance at Dumouriez as a Girondist partisan, and became now more convinced than ever that he was working in the interest of the faction, and that the defeat was due to treachery, The Girondin ministers and generals were the objects of the bitterest resentment. So high did the feeling run that a conspiracy was set on foot to assassinate the leading men of the party in the Convention on the night of the 10th of March. The conspirators, it is alleged, actually set out, but the plan miscarried, owing to its betrayal beforehand to the persons threatened. Vergniaud, the great Girondin orator denounced the plot next day in the Assembly, and the advanced parties were for a moment checked. But the news of the spread of the aristocratic revolt it the district of the Loire known as La Vendée, quickly enabled them to regain their ascendancy. The Vendée was a district in which there were no large towns and, consequently hardly any middle-class or proletariat. It was a district inhabited almost exclusively by peasants, priests, and nobles, and consequently altogether out of touch with the objects of the Revolution. The peasantry still venerated their old masters, and hated the new middle-class. The immediate cause of the outbreak however, was the fresh levy in Paris. The feeling against "Moderates" and half-hearted friends of the Republic waxed greater than ever. The new Revolutionary Tribunal redoubled its activity. Following upon the bad news from the Vendée came that of further and still more serious reverses in Belgium on the part of Dumouriez, and; what was worse, indisputable evidence of intrigues with the Austrians to establish the monarchy in the person of the Duc de Chartres, the young son of Phillipe d'Orleans Egalité (the King's cousin and a member of the Mountain party). This Duc de Chartres, at that time a lieutenant of Dumouriez, became subsequently "Louis Philippe, King of the French." Dumouriez almost immediately after openly proclaimed his intention of marching upon Paris to subdue the Revolution. But he did not succeed any better than Lafayette, his predecessor in the same course. His troops, although attached to him personally, hesitated at treachery to the Republic. The same with the officers. Meanwhile the Convention was energetic; it sent four commissioners, among them the Minister of War, to summon the traitor general to the bar of the Convention. He not only refused to come, but handed over the commissioners as hostages to the Austrians. After a further fruitless attempt to seduce the army he sought refuge with the Duc de Chartres and a few other officers in the Austrian camp, and from this time history knows him no more. Dumouriez's defection drove the last nail into the coffin of the Girondist power. There is a well-known proverb that those whom the gods would destroy they first make mad. This was certainly exemplified in the present case. For the Girondins had already, before their General Dumouriez's escape had become known, alienated the leading Mountainist who had been in favour of reconciliation. between the parties – Danton, to wit – by unsubstantiated insinuations. And note, when Dumouriez's desertion had been for days past a topic of discussion and declamation amongst the Paris sections. They succeeded amid scenes of violent disorder in the Convention in getting a decree of indictment launched against Marat on the ground of the paragraph about the forestallers. The "People's Friend" was accordingly brought before the Revolutionary Tribunal, the Girondists vainly attempting to pack the jury. After a trial lasting two days he was acquitted amid the acclamations of the audience, and carried in triumph by the populace into the hall of the Convention. Girondism was henceforth plainly a lost cause so far as peaceful and legal action was concerned. Its only hope lay in an insurrection of the departments. This also, as we shall see, was destined to failure. Meanwhile Custine, Damprière, and their generals were sent to reorganise the armies of Dumouiiez, but for the next few weeks the main attention of all patriots was directed to one object – the destruction of the Girondist faction.

Concerning Matters Economic

Amid all this contention the Mountain, aided by economic pressure, succeeded in forcing through some important administration, and two great economic measures. In addition to the "Revolutionary Tribunal" two powerful committees were established which, in the end, practically assumed all the executive functions of a dictatorial ministry. These were the "Committee of General Security," consisting of twenty-one members, and the "Committee of Public Safety," consisting of nine members. The economic measures referred: to were, first, the Law of Maximum, by means of which, at a stroke, the starvation and misery previously existing were allayed. The law of maximum enacted a fixed price for bread-stuffs, above which it was penal to sell them. To avert the possibility of the dealers refusing to sell at all, it was made compulsory upon them to do so. They were, moreover, obliged to furnish accurate accounts of their stock, which could, if desirable be peremptorily "checked" by the authorities. The law was subsequently extended to all the necessaries of life. The other economic measure forced through the Convention by the Jacobins and the Mountain was a progressive income-tax on an ascending scale. In, addition to these there was a forced loan of a milliard for war purposes, levied on the wealthy classes. The Girondists and the Plain, of course, shrieked and kicked at these glaring infringements of the "laws" of political economy and the rights of property; but the middle-class factions, though nominally dominant, were not really so, and were hence unable to resist the force of the popular demand for decisive steps in the direction of greater economic equality.

The law of maximum and the progressive income-tax are the only two measures of a directly Socialist tendency which have ever been practically applied, and with complete success. And yet it is strange that at least the first of these measures, when proposed now-a-days, is viewed by many Socialists with indifference, not to say suspicion. It only shows how, in economics, as in other things, the rags of old superstitions unconsciously survive in us. Those who have triumphed over the old-fashioned bourgeois fallacies of the wickedness and inutility of interfering with the sacred laws of political economy by direct legislative interference with the freedom of production, still wince at the notion of direct legislative interference with freedom (so-called) of exchange. An eight-hour law is an excellent thing, but a maximum, by which the eight-hour workman is protected from the extortions of monopoly and the power of industrial and commercial capital to raise prices, guarding itself against the effects of competition by "rings" and "corners" – this is a very doubtful thing indeed! .In the present day of course, a law of maximum would be of very little use unless supplemented by a law of minimum, i.e. a law fixing a minimum wage, and, we may add, parenthetically, the, eight hours working day would in all probability also prove itself a questionable boon if unaccompanied by both these provisos. But in France at the end of the last century it was not so. That petite industrie, prevailed everywhere except in the large towns where the workshop system had obtained a footing, though even there without having by any means entirely supplanted the smaller production. The law of maximum alone was therefore sufficient to meet all requirements. Scarcity and want there was still, but it was a scarcity and want due, for the most part to other than remediable social conditions. Bad harvests, the devastations of foreign invasion and civil war had reduced France to the lowest ebb. The law of maximum saved it. With the two francs a day which was voted at a subsequent period as the allowance of every attendant at the primary assemblies of the sections or wardships of which there were 44,000 in all France the problem of the unemployed was solved, for the nonce, Th, number of the unemployed in all trades ministering to the luxuries of the rich may be imagined, and a measure of this kind absolutely essential.

The net result of the interference by the Convention with the "laws of Political Economy" is well expressed by Carlyle (vii. 6), where he declares that "there is no period to be met with, in which the general 25,000,000 of France suffered less than in this period, which they name reign of terror." Time was as yet not ripe for the great constructive movement of modern Socialism; and hence the merely remedial treatment here explained was all that could even be attempted. The great fact to be noted is that for the first time in history the cry for material and. social equality as opposed to mere political and legal equality became definitely articulate. That cry has often enough since been smothered, but has always made itself heard again at short intervals. The party of the Mountain and Sanscullottism, the Babeuf conspiracy, the Chartist movement the days of June, 1848, the Commune of 1871 are all so many stages in the awakening of the Proletariat to the full consciousness of itself which it attains in Modern Socialism.

The Fall of the Gironde

Apart from the laws referred to in the last chapter, which were with difficulty forced through the Legislature by the Mountain, the six weeks which elapsed between the acquittal of Marat and the 2nd of June, the day of the extinction of the Girondist power, were fruitful in nothing but a progressive mutual exacerbation of the two parties. Petitions and deputations began to pour in praying for the expulsion and even condemnation of some twenty-two of the leading Girondists. On the 10th of May the Convention shifted its quarters from the old Riding School to the Tuilleries. The avenues to the new convention hall were continually blocked by sansculottes (the breechless), the name given to the party of the people since the émeute of the 21st of June, 1792, when a pair of black breeches was paraded in token of the want of these commodities by the working classes of France. At last the Girondins made up their .minds for a dashing stroke. Guadet suddenly moved the immediate suppression of the Commune, its piece to be filled ad interim by the presidents of the sections, the transference of the legislation to Bourges with the smallest possible delay, and the despatch of the decree into the provinces by expresses. The Mountain was taken unawares, and it is possible, if the Girondists had had the courage to proceed to action immediately, they might have been successful. But this they did not dare do in face of the urgency of the situation on the frontier, well-knowing that civil war would be the outcome. Indeed, it is doubtful whether they could have in any case obtained a majority in the Assembly under the circumstances. Barrere proposed, as a compromise, the establishment of a commission of twelve members to enquire into the conduct of the municipality, to search out the plots of the Jacobins, and to arrest suspected persons. The proposition was accepted, and the commission established. Under the pretence of having discovered a new conspiracy it immediately proceeded to imprison several prominent persons, among them being the secretary of the Commune, Hébert, editor of the Père Duchesne newspaper, This at once excited immense popular indignation. Deputation followed deputation demanding Hébert's release. The Commune, the Mountainist mayor, Paché, at its head, placed itself in permanent connection with the committees of the sections, which, together with the clubs of the Jacobins and Cordeliers; declared themselves in permanent session.

On the 27th of May the rising of Paris against the Convention began. The Commune presented itself before the Convention in a body, demanding the release of its chief secretary, and the suppression of the Girondist commission. Deputies from the sections followed, all calling for its suppression, and some for the arrest of its members. The Girondist president, Isnard, met these demands with the threat that the departmems should be raised and Pacts annihilates, so that "the wayfarer would have to enquire on which side of the Seine Paris had stood," a reply which became the signal for a general revolt of the Mountain.

The hall was now the scene of violent confusion in which swords and pistols were drawn (and during which the crowd poured in, the upshot being that Isnard was compelled to leave the chair and make way for the Mountainist and friend of Danton, Hérault de Séchelles. Hérault at once replied, conceding the demands of the petitioners.

The Mountain had won the day, Hébert's arrest was annulled, sad the commission suppressed amid the acclamation of the populace. The next day the Girondists, with suicidal folly, succeeded by a scratch majority in re-establishing the Commission on the ground that the proceedings of the previous day had been irregular. A veritable yell of indignation from clubs, sections and municipality greeted this resolution. Robespierre, Danton, Marat, Chaumette .and Paché constituted themselves into an informal committee to organise anew the movement. On the 30th the clubs and sections publicly declared themselves in a state of insurrection, their delegates, to the number of ninety-six, entering the Hotel de Ville, and as a matter of form annulling the municipality (as a legally constituted body), but immediately reinstating its members in their functions under insurrectionary auspices. Mayor Paché was sent to report the matter to the Convention, while Henriot, the new commandant of the National Guard, called upon the sections to be ready for action at any moment, the sansculottes to be allowed two francs a day so long as they remained under orders. Early the following morning, the 31st, the tocsin was rung and the générale beat and the armed sections were assembled and marched upon the Tuilleries.

The signal for the insurrection was an alarm cannon which was fired just as Mayor Paché was making his report, and, it must be admitted, trying to hoodwink the legislature with the pretence that he was not privy to the proceedings. The consternation in the assembly at the ominous sound was general. Danton rushed to the tribune to demand anew the suppression of the Commission. All the leading Mountainists did the same. The majority still hesitated. Deputations now began to arrive thick and fast, till all the gangways were now blocked up by excited crowds. The suppression of the Commission and the arrest of its members, and of the other leading Girondists, was loudly demanded on all sides. Various propositions were being discussed when the report spread that the Tuilleries was surrounded by armed forces and the Convention no longer' free. Even some members of the Mountain winced at this "outrage" on the "national sovereignty." At length it was decided that the Assembly should march out in a body and confront the insurgents. This was done, Hérault de Séchelles leading the way. They were met by Henriot on horseback at the head of the armed bands, brandishing a sabre. "The people want not phrases," said he, "but the arrest of twenty-two traitors."

Two-cannon were immediately pointed straight at the Convention, which prudently retired. All the other exits from the Tuilleries Gardens were found to bristle equally with pikes and sabres, so there was nothing for it but to go back again into the hall. The popular demands were no longer opposed. Marat, who had been the life and soul of the whole movement throughout, now dictated the names of the proscribed and the form of the resolution from the tribune. All the leading Girondins, including the twelve forming the Commission were placed under arrest. Upon the result being known outside, the insurgents quickly dispersed. Thus perished Girondism. Ever since the 10th of August the nominal power in the state had been in the hands of the Girondist party, although as we have seen, the real power was very far from being so. Henceforth they were a proscribed faction, whose members at last thought themselves lucky if they could find a corner of France in which to conceal themselves.

The Sansculottes in Power

The Girondists, driven successively from the Jacobins Club, the Municipality (where Petion had for long been replaced in the mayoralty by Paché), and finally from the Convention, now played out their last card, the attempt to raise the Provinces, which were largely with them. Never was the position of France more desperate than at this moment. "La Vendée" in open and hitherto successful insurrection on one side, the coalition of Europe again pouring in its levies on three sides, and a Girondist insurrection brewing at several points in the interior. The Girondists, after their defeat in Paris, tried to rally at Caen, in Normandy, which town became the head quarters of the conspiracy as long as it lasted. Negotiations were entered into with General Wimpfen and a Royalist; one Comte Puisaye. Somehow, in spite of the sympathy of the departments, especially the large middle-class towns, the project failed completely as a general movement, partly owing to mismanagement, want of concert and Royalist intrigues which alienated many otherwise sympathetic, partly to the presence of the foreign invader, and partly owing to the vigorous action of the leaders of the Revolution in Paris. The provinces hesitated, the insurgents dispersed, a few towns in the south only remained to the Girondins. The insurrection did not miscarry for want of tall talk, it is certain, or the Girondins as usual were eloquent in threats couched in well-rounded periods.

While this was going on a young woman of "good" family in Caen, who had been largely in the society of Girondins, and had heard much talk of Marat as the leader of the recent movement, without stating her intention to anybody, travelled up to Paris by diligente, and obtaining an interview with the popular leader under the pretext of furnishing information of the conspiracy at Caen, murdered him. Poor Marat, who was almost dying at the time, was in a bath; his helpless condition rendering him an easy prey for the knife of his dastardly assassin. A few sous only were found in his possession.

Thus perished the first great vindicator of the rights of the modern Proletariat, a truly single-minded champion of the oppressed. Of average intellect merely, it is Marat's unique and titanic. force of character which must make him immortal in history.

Charlotte Corday was tried and condemned before the Revolutionary tribunal; maintaining a theatrical demeanour to the last. She was guillotined on the 17th of July, three days after the assassination. A poor fool, a native of Mainz; Adam Lutz by name, went crazy over her.

The death of the "people's friend" caused a veritable panic in the ranks of the Revolutionary party. No "patriot" was without some token of him. He was invoked in every revolutionary function, and his bust was crowned in all public assemblies. The convention unanimously granted him the honours of the Pantheon. The fugitive Girondins now found their position harder than ever. They had to fly from Caen before the emissane of the Convention. Jacobin commissions were scouring the country up and down, the Revolutionary power in Paris having developed an almost superhuman activity. The only places where the insurrection still flickered on was in Lyons, Marseilles, and Bordeaux, cities which had compromised themselves too far, to hope for forgiveness from the convention, and which (notably Lyons) were destined before long to feel the heavy hand of Sanscullottic vengeance.

Yet notwithstanding the virtual collapse of the Girondist rebellion the state of affairs had hardly improved. The armies now again everywhere on the defensive were disorganised and dispirited. Things still seemed utterly hopeless. If France was to be saved it could only by a dead lift. The revolutionary power in Paris now consisted of the convention (or rather the Mountain, which dominated the whole assembly), the two committees (of General Security and of Public Safety), the Commune, or Municipality, and, lastly, the clubs of the Jacobins and Cordeliers, especially the former, whose deliberations were hardly second in importance to those of the Convention. The primary assemblies of the forty-eight sections, in which every citizen was free to express his opinion, were also a considerable factor in public affairs.

This agglomeration of popular forces constituted the power which had to raise France and the Revolution out of the abyss into which they had sunk. The consolidation of the new government was the first thing to he attempted. The long talked-of constitution was next put in hand; Hérault de Séchelles being entrusted with the task of drawing it up. This celebrated constitution of '93, for long regarded as the sheet-anchor of Sanscullottism, is probably the most thoroughgoing scheme of pure democracy ever devised. It not only formally recognised the people, as the sole primary source of power, but it delegated the exercise of that power directly to them. Every measure was to be submitted to the primary assemblies of which there were forty-four thousand in all France. The magistrates were to be re-elected at the shortest possible intervals by simple majority. The central legislature was to be renewed annually, consisting of delegates from the primary assemblies who were to be furnished with imperative mandates.

This constitution passed the Convention and was accepted by a large majority of the wardships throughout France. The representatives of the said forty-four thousand wardships when they came to the Convention demanded in face of the existing emergency "he arrest of all suspected persons and a general rising of the people." Danton in a vigorous speech moved that the Commissioners of the primary assemblies should be instructed to report the state of arms, provisions, and ammunition, and to raise a levy of four hundred thousand men, and that the Convention should take the oath of death or victory. This was carried unanimously. A few days after, Barrere, in the name of the committees, proposed still more decisive measures. All the male population from eighteen to twenty-five were placed under arms; and new requisitions were made. Soon there were forty armies, comprising in all 1,200,000 men. The Committee of Public Safety, with Carnot (grandfather. of the present President of the French Republic) chief of the War Department, were untiring in their energies at home and abroad. Forty sous a day, was enacted as the allowance of every sectionist: The famous Law of Suspects was passed, and wholesale arrests were made of persons thought to be of Girondist or Royalist sympathies. The middle-classes fared now as badly as the aristocracy had previously. The reign of Terror had begun, necessitated by the same exigencies as the September Massacres – imminent foreign invasion combined with domestic treachery. As before, the moment decisive action was taken, matters began to mend on all sides, though Toulon was in the hands of the English, Marseilles and Boulogne was taken from the Girondin immigrants and Lyons besieged. The Constitution, although carried, was suspended in face of the emergency, and as a matter of fact was never put into force.

The Dictatorship of the Commune

The revolutionary power in Paris, as we have said, was nominally divided between the Commune, at the head of which were Hébert and Chaumette, the two committees, which included Robespierre, Danton, Carnot, &c., the Convention, and the – Jacobin's Club, whose influence, though unofficial and indirect, was in no respect less than that of the representative assembly itself. During the period from August 10th, 1792, to the fall of the Girondins the centre of power lay in the Convention; in the period from the 2nd of June, 1793, to the 24th of March, 1794 (the fall of Hébert), it resided mainly in the Commune; from the 24th of March to the 27th of July, 1794 (the fall of Robespierre), it was the committees especially the Committee of Public Safety, which practically dictated to France. The Jacobin's club meanwhile reflected for the most part the attitude of the dominant Parisian opinion, and of the governing body. It underwent several épurations, or purifications, in the course of the revolutionary period, on which occasions a batch of members, whose views were out of accord with the prevalent feeling of the hour, would be expelled.

Almost simultaneously with the collapse of the Girondist rising and the entry of the Convention – troops into the cities of the, south, the tide begun to turn in La Vendée; the attempt of the insurgents to take Nantes failed, and though the insurrection lingered on for some time longer it never again became formidable. The evolutionary armies, indeed, were nearly everywhere victorious under the new generals, Moreau, Hoche, Pichegru, Jourdan, Kellermann, &c. The Prussians and Austrians, under the command of the Prince of Coburg, were dislodged from their vantage-ground in the east ; the Spaniards in the south, and the English and Hanoverians in the north. Thus a second time was France, by stupendous dead-lift effort, saved from imminent ruin by the raw levies of the revolution.

The victories of Dumouriez in '92 were repeated on a grander scale in the great campaign, which the genius of Carnot "organised" in '93 and '94. The revolution now was answering the coalition is the spirit of Danton's defiant menace "the combined kings threaten us, we hurl at their, feet as gage of battle the head of a king." France was converted into one vast camp. But for many months yet the French were not destined to feel themselves "out of the wood." The dread of possible reverses followed by invasion and political extinction was ever before their eyes. And hence it was not till the end of July, '94 that the reaction against "the terror" had gathered strength enough to overthrow the system itself.

So long as danger threatened from without public opinion tolerated the guillotine, and at the period at which we have arrived the greatest activity of that famous instrument began. The "law of the suspect," which enabled the committees of the sections to arrest all suspected persons and incarcerate them prior to their being brought before the Revolutionary Tribunal, speedily filled the prisons to overflowing. After conviction and death the property of the executed was confiscated to the State. The commune was the virtual head of the revolutionary committees of the sections in the provinces as welt as in Paris. The National Guard was under its orders, and it had flying columns in its pay scouring different parts of the country. The Commune may be taken as the representative in the revolution of the proletarian interest, pure and simple. Though the circumstances of the time caused it to be unhappily an instrument of the Terror, its activity was by no means confined to this. The Commune made it pretty soon evident that in its eyes the existence of a commercial middle-class was quite as incompatible with the welfare of the people as that of an aristocracy.

Economical equality was the avowed end of the revolution for the Commune. Hébert and Chaumette nevertheless busied themselves with various projects of a palliative character, such as hospital and prison reform. They attempted to introduce primary and secular education into every village n France. The law of maximum (and compulsory sale) was at their suggestion enlarged in scope, being applied to almost all articles of common .consumption. Forestalling was forbidden under the heaviest penalties. A maximum was even applied to wages at this time (a proceeding calculated in a society not yet out of the small production to make considerable havoc with what some people call the "rent of ability," though it was enacted solely with a view to government employment for the national defence. The Bourse was closed. Financial and commercial syndicates were dissolved. The paper money, or assignats, were made compulsory tender at their nominal value.

On the 5th of October the new republican calendar, the joint work of the astronomer Romme, who furnished the calculations, and the clever fuilletonist Fabre d'Eglantine, who supplied the poetical nomenclature, came into operation. The new era was to date from the declaration of the Republic, the 21st of September, 1792, so that the months do riot coincide with those of the ordinary calendar. The three autumn months were Vendemiaire, or the vintage month, Brumaire, or the foggy month, and Frimaire, or the frosty month; the three winter months, Nivose, or the snowy month, Pluviose, or the rainy month, and Ventose, or the windy month; the three spring months, Germinal, or the budding month, Forêal, or the flowery month, and Prairial, or the meadowy month; and the three summer months, Messidor, or the reaping month, Thermidor, or the heating month, and Fructidor, or the fruiting month. The week of seven days was abolished and decades or periods of ten days instituted instead.

But the work for which the Commune is most famous is the establishment of the new Cultus – the Worship of Reason. The Hébertists, as the party of the Commune were called, and among whom was Anarcharsis Clootz, were rightly convinced that deliverance from the dogmas of supernatural religion was the necessary complement of deliverance from the thraldom of privilege and wealth. In accordance with 18th century habits of thought, and especially French 18th century thought, with its classicism, the idea naturally suggested itself of initiating a worship of Reason as personified, on the ruins of God, Christ and the Virgin. For some time past, stimulated by the missionaries of the Commune, numbers of priests had been sending in their demissions declaring they would no longer preach a lie, and that Liberty and the public welfare was their only God. The church plate in every part of France was melted down for patriotic uses, vestments, bibles, and breviaries made bonfires, to the accompaniment of the "Carmagnole." Early in November Gobel, the Archbishop of Paris, together with his chapter, entered the Convention-hall to publicly renounce the Christian faith. Christian rites and worship were now proscribed, and a Festival of Reason was decreed by the Commune at the instance proscribed, and a Festival of was decreed by the Commune at the instance of Chaumette. A few days later, and a procession of citizens and citoyennes, in priestly vestments and other fantastic costumes, followed by mules and barrows laden with church furniture, defiled into the Convention, and after chanting strophes to Reason, proceeded to dance the "Carmagnole," many of the legislators taking part. Later on the same day, Procureur Chaumette, at the head of the Commune and the presidents of sections, arrived bearing in their midst, on a palaquin, Mlle Candeille, the danseuse, in bonnet rouge and blue mantle; garlanded with oak, as the Goddess of Reason. The bulk of the Convention then rose, and after giving the goddess the; formal kiss, proceeded in a body to Notre Dame where the new worship was inaugurated amid music, tricolour, and virgins dressed is white. A similar ceremony with other goddesses, took place at St. Eustache, and other of the principal churches of Paris. Commissioners soon established the new worship throughout the length and breadth of French territory, from Antwerp in the north to Marseilles in the south. In place of the mass the old cathedrals re-echoed to strophes in honour of Reason and in praise of "Liberty, Equality, and Fraternity." Old things had passed away, and all things had become new.

The Terror

By means of its courageous contempt for the so-called lays of political economy and the compulsion exercised on all traders and, farmers, with the aid of its "revolutionary army," to sell at the maximum price, the fearful want occasioned by the circumstances of the time was kept under to a considerable extent by the Commune. The revolutionary committees established in every section of France, the ambulatory deputies who watched the provinces and were present with the military forces, and last, but not least, the army of the Commune under General Ronsin, nevertheless had hard work to prevent the law of maximum from being violated. Arrests in Paris and the provinces went on apace. The Commune now granted a free allowance of bread for each family. By the end of October 3,000 persons were in the prisons of Paris alone. The revolutionary committees had power to arrest all persons suspected of reactionary tendencies.

On the 14th of October the queen, Marie Antoinette, was brought before the revolutionary tribunal and convicted, after two days hearing, on overwhelming evidence, of the basest treachery towards France, and of the most sanguinary intentions with regard to Paris. It was, indeed, high time that this atrocious woman met her deserts. When the country was at the lowest depths of misery some years before the outbreak of the revolution, all this abandoned wretch could think of was squandering fabulous sums of the nation's wealth, in conjunction with her friend, the court head prostitute and procuress, the Princess de Lamballe (killed in the September massacres), on jewels, balls, and sinecures for her paramours. If anyone ventured to call attention to some flagrant abuse in her presence he was invariably silenced with the reply, "Yes, but we must amuse ourselves" (Oui mais il faut s'amuser). It was only after her amusements had been curtailed by the utter collapse of the finances, a consummation to which she had contributed so largely by her criminal extravagances, that she began to interest herself in public affairs. Her aim was then to get back the means for her debaucheries, and when the revolution broke out and affairs looked less and less productive of diamond necklaces, &c., her hatred against the new regime which had deprived her of those things knew no bounds, and henceforth her one hope was a foreign invasion, which would quench the revolution in the blood of France, and place the French people once more in her power. As for poor, feeble foolish Louis, he was completely in the toils of this noxious reptile. (1) Many who looked on at the tumbril conveying her to execution must have been inclined to think that the guillotine was too good for the foul Autrichienne.

She was not without certain histrionic ability, and when before the tribunal played out her "womanhood" in a manner which showed that she might have gained an honest living in transpontine melodrama. Much indignation has been expended, on the charge of misconduct towards her son, the little dauphin, which Hébert, brought against her. It is sufficient here to state that there are extant documents which show that the charge was not made without very good grounds; although in the nature of things it could not be certainly proved. The fact is it is a mistake to apply the ordinary canons of motherhood .to a creature like Marie Antoinette. She was altogether an obscene misbirth of the corrupt court-life of the 18th century, the like of which, let us hope, may never be seen again.

Apropos of the dauphin, it is necessary to caution our readers against the lies the reaction anent his treatment, and especially the foul calumnies against the young shoemaker, Simon, in whose care he was placed: All the contemporary evidence goes to show that the poor child received every consideration and kindness, but that having inherited a scrofulous or syphilitic constitution from both parents, which was further weakened in ways unnecessary to go into, it was impossible to rear him, and in spite of every care he died in the Temple, the following year.

On the 24th of October the 22 Girondists were brought to trial.

They were convicted after five days' proceedings, and guillotined on the 6th. Valaze, one of their number, stabbed himself to death with a dagger on hearing the sentence, but his body was nevertheless sent to be guillotined with the rest. They embraced each other on arriving at the "Place de la Revolution," and died singing the Marseillaise. Proofs of their complicity in the insurrection of the departments were complete. They had played for high stakes and lost. Seventy-three other Girondist deputies had been for some time under lock and key, having been compromised in some papers found at the house of a deputy whom Charlotte Corday had visited on her first arrival in Paris. With the execution of the 22, however, Girondism, as a distinct party, finally disappears from history. The Girondins, it may here be mentioned, were largely under the influence of Voltaire, just as the Mountain as a party was chiefly under the influence of Rousseau. Meanwhile Lyons, the last stronghold of Royalism and Girondism, had fallen, and Toulon had been recovered from the English, to whom it had been surrendered. Both towns were visited with a fearful vengeance. Collot d'Herbois, who was a member both of the Commune and of the Committee of Public Safety, ordered wholesale massacres of the inhabitants of the former city in his capacity of Commissioner. Billaud-Varennes, a colleague of Collot's, was also a leading agent of the terror in provinces. At Nantes, Carrier, another Commissioner, inaugurated his horrible Noyades, or drownings, in which those suspected of Royalism or moderation were placed in boats with false bottoms and drowned in the Loire. In some of these cases a man and woman were tied together naked. This was called "republican marriage." All these things were very infamous, it will be said, and so they were. But they were not any worse, if so bad, as the acts of more than one respectable government in '48, of the Czar in Poland in '65, or of the Versaillists in Paris to '71, events which the middle-classes have complacently swallowed without indignation.

Note

1. The real character of Marie Antoinette, apart from the lies of Royalist historians, may be seen from her correspondence with Maria Theresa, and of the latter with the Comte Mercy d'Argenteau. A good digest of it is given in M. Georges Avenel's essay, La vrai Marie Antoinette.

The Fall of the Hébertists

After the 10th of August and the events that arose out of it of which he was the heart and soul, Danton had proved something of a failure. His peace negotiations with England had led to nothing, his attempts at reconciliation between Mountain and Gironde had likewise proved abortive; he had played no important part since the 31st of May in the Convention itself, and finally retired with his young wife for some weeks in disgust to his native town of Arcis sur Aube, whence he returned some time after to join his friend Camille Desmoulins in attacking the system of the terror. It should be explained that the Cordeliers Club, of which Danton had formerly been the head, had been reconstituted some time since, and was now entirely composed of Hébertists. Camille, at the beginning of December, started a new journal called The Old Cordelier, which attacked the terrorists and especially the Commune with bitter sarcasm. At first Robespierre approved of the sentiments there expressed, and even looked over and corrected the proofs of the first numbers. It pleased him, possibly, that the Hébertists were sharply attacked. For the pedantic Rousseauite prig Robespierre, was mortally offended with the atheism of the party of the Commune, and had recently been delivering violent harangues, against the worship of Reason, at the Jacobins' Club. There was also an old standing jealousy on the part of the Committee of Public Safety with the Commune on account of the influence the latter wielded with the aid of its "revolutionary army." Nevertheless Robespierre's two colleagues on the committee, Billaud Varennes and Collot D'Herbois, were enraged at the idea of even mitigating "the terror", and the notion found but little support generally. Robespierre, whose influence was now immense, became alarmed lest he should be tarred with moderation, and hence a coolness sprang up between him and his friend Camille and the other Dantonists.

Meanwhile he guillotine was working steadily, and some noteworthy heads were failing or had lately fallen. Among them we may notice Philippe D'Orleans Egalité, the ex-member of the Mountain and the king's cousin, arrested at the time Dumouriez's intrigues with his son became known, and decreed accused along with the Girondins, but not convicted till later. In November Madame Roland was also put on her trial. She was condemned, and went to the Place de la Revolution by the side of a poor printer, whom she endeavoured to console. Arrived there she asked for paper and ink to write down "the strange thoughts that were arising within her." She died with real heroism. It can only be regretted that a woman of so many fine qualities should have allowed herself to be so blinded by party fanaticism as to pen the slanders against the leaders of the Mountain which stain her Memoirs, Her Girondism may have been a. matter of honest conviction, but it is hard to believe that many of these calumnies were not deliberate inventions.

Bailly, the first mayor of Paris under the new régime, him of the red flag of the Champ de Mars, in July, 1791, was one of the executed. Barnard, the constitutionalist leader in the

Constituent Assembly, also suffered. The corpse of the Girondist Pétion, who succeeded Bailly in the mayoralty of Paris, was found, about this time in a wood near St. Emilion, partly devoured by wolves. The heads of ex-ministers and generals were falling by the score.

But to return to the contest of parties in the government. Put in a few words, the matter stood as follows: on one side were the Hébertists, representing the Commune and the Terror; on the opposite were the Dantonists, representing to a large extent the Mountain or Convention party, hostile to both the commune and the terror, wishing to see the constitution established and the Convention all powerful. Between the two were the committees that of "public safety" being the dominant one. The committeemen were mostly hostile to the power of the Commune which stood in their way, but were determined to maintain the system of the terror, and not to let the Convention override them.

Robespierre, after some hesitation ranged himself on the side of his committee alike against the Dantonists, with whom he had, up till now, been friendly, and the Hebertists, to whom he had been always more or less hostile. The struggle lasted between three and four months. Since the reconstitution of the Committee of Public Safety in July, when Billaud and Collot came into it, the Dantonists had had no influence on either of the committees. The attack on the Hebertist's was begun by the suppression of the revolutionary armies in the provinces, and a decree forbidden the sending of agents into the provinces by the Commune, and this was followed up in inside and outside the Convention by attacks on every action of the commune from the Dantonists and the mountain, and from the committees. The Jacobins' Club continued to be the battle-ground between Robespierre and the Hébertists. Then Robespierre thundered nightly against atheistic intolerance, said that atheism was aristocratic, on the logical ground that certain aristocrats had been atheists, just as though anyone were to argue that Socialism couldn't be Secularistic because Mr. Bradlaugh is a Secularist. He maundered about the necessity of a supreme being as the avenger of injured innocence, &c.

At last the compact between Robespierre and his fellow committee men, Billaud and Collot, was struck. They were to surrender the Hébertists while he was to surrender the Dantonists. Accordingly Hébert, Ronsin, Vincent, Clootz, Momoro, &c., already expelled from the Jacobins club were arrested, and after a mock trial, in which they here accused of taking money from the English Government to discredit the Republic by their excesses were, on March 24th, 1794, sent to the guillotine. Poor Chaumette's turn came a few days later. A week afterwards Danton. who had come back to Paris at the earnest solicitation of his friends, and had sought ineffectually to compromise matters with Robespierre, was sent before the revolutionary tribunal. His oratory was nearly securing his acquittal when Robespierre got a special law hurried through the Convention which closed his mouth, and he, too, went his way in company with Camille Desmoulins, Phillipeaux, Herault de Sechelles and others, to the Place de la Revolution. Thus was the revolution, indeed, like Saturn, devouring its own children.

When we first came across Robespierre he was, although a prig and a repulsive prig at that, apparently actuated by as much honesty of purpose as any other leader. His services to the revolution at all the great crises were real. But the germ of ambition and personal self-seeking, which was always observable, grew with the progress of events, until, at the period we have now reached, he had developed into a monster, possessed of one aim – to become dictator, and prepared to make any sacrifice whatever for the accomplishment of that aim. The murder of friends like Danton and Camille Desmoulins, with whom he had lived and worked on terms of close intimacy since the beginning of the revolution, yields to nothing in history for its treachery and infamy.

The Rule of Robespierre.

The Commune was now overthrown, and all independence stifled in the Convention, No initiative remained but that of the Committee of Public Safety, and in the Committee itself little, at least, in internal affairs, but that of Robespierre and his partisans. The chief among the latter were Couthon and Lebas in Paris, and St. Just as Commissioner in the provinces. The municipality, now that most of the old members were guillotined or expelled, was filled up with subordinate creatures of Robespierre. A Belgian architect, named Fleariot-Lescot replaced the sincere and noble-minded Pache as mayor of Paris. The same sort of thing went on all round. Robespierre had succeeded in reducing the Jacobins' Club to a mere claque of his own. The Convention was not much better. A look from the "Incorruptible" sufficed to frown down all opposition.

The increase of the terror now became frightful all over France, but especially in Paris. Robespierre himself directed the police department. On the 22nd of Prairial (the 10th of June), as atrocious law was passed at the instigation of the dictator, whereby persons sent before the Revolutionary Tribunal, now divided into four sections, were refused the right of defence. This meant, of course, that whereas before about a third of those accused were acquitted, henceforth all prisoners were condemned, when nothing else could be alleged against them, on the general and vague charge of "conspiracies in the prisons." Men and women were now tried by the public prosecutor, Fouquier Tinville, and the judges of the Tribunal, in batches of fifty or sixty at once. It would be a mistake to suppose that it was chiefly the well-to-do that suffered. On the contrary, out of 2,750 victims of Robespierre's, only 650 belonged to the upper or middle classes. The tumbrils that wended their way daily to the Place de la Revolution were largely filled with workingmen. During the last three weeks of the tyrants rule, 1,125 persons were executed in Paris alone. Thus did this criminal monster drown the Revolution itself in the blood of his victims. Marat had already foreseen the results of Robespierre's self-idolatry, when during a speech of the latter in the Convention, he whispered to his neighbour Dubois-Cranci, "with such doctrines as that he will do more harm than all the tyrants put together."

The notion of becoming the high-priest of a new religion had been working in Robespierre's mind ever since the fall of the Hébertists. After many speeches in the Jacobins' Club, Maximilian at last, on the 18th of May, mounted the Convention tribune to demand that it be decreed that "the French. people recognises the existence of a Supreme Being and the immortality of the soul," and that a festival should be held in the honour of such Being. In his speech, he dwelt on the distinction between a pure Deism and the superstitious cults of priests, said that it mattered not whether the existence of God were demonstrated or even probable, that in the eyes of the legislator all is truth which is useful in the world and in practice," and that a god was an indispensable article of state-furniture, and much more to the same effect.

Deputations from the new Robespierrised Commune, from the Jacobins, and from the sections next filed in with the petition that the Convention should vouchsafe to grant them a God and immortality. The resolution was carried amid thunders of applause in the same Convention which six months previously had applauded the atheistic worship of Reason. A few days later one undoubted; and another more questionable, attempt at assassination were made. The first on Collot D'Herbois, on the steps of his house; and the second on Robespierre himself by a young woman named Cécile Rinault. Robespierre was out when she called, but she was arrested, and knives were found in her possession. She was guilliotined, together with all her family. Fifty-four persons were involved in this execution, which took place in the Faubourg St. Antoine, the great workmen's quarter.

At last the eventful day, the 20th of Prairial (8th of June), fixed for the glorification of the Supreme Being, arrived. The Convention, the Jacobins, and Sections in gala attire, might have been seen wending their way through the Tuilleries' gardens, the procession headed by Robespierre, radiant in sky-blue coat and black breeches, bearing in his hand an enormous bunch of corn, fruits, and flowers, a classical touch suggested by the pagan functions of antiquity. Arrived at an artificial altar, on the top of which were allegorical figures intended to represent Atheism, Anarchy, &c., Robespierre proceeded to set fire to the latter with a torch. They blazed away, and presently by a triumph of mechanical art the Supreme-Being himself emerged from their ashes, rather the worse for smoke, it is said. The "Incorruptible" made three harangues, but the hopes of those who expected an announcement of a cessation of the Terror were damped when he proclaimed: "To-day, let us enjoy ourselves, to-morrow begin afresh to fight the enemies of the Revolution." All knew what this meant, and two days later the monstrous law before spoken of was passed, and the Terror entered upon its last and acutest stage. This disappointment of the public hopes was the beginning of the fall of Robespierre's popularity outside the governing bodies. Suppressed hatred and jealousy of him had long been the growing feeling in the Convention, while on the Committee of Public Safety he had become at loggerheads with all except his own henchmen. The law of Prairial was the last occasion that the Committee appeared united before the Convention. So strained were their relations that Robespierre henceforth rarely attended the sittings of the Committee, and appeared comparatively seldom in the Convention itself, leaving everything to Couthon, St. Just, and Lebas. On the other hand, he was assiduous in his attendance at the Jacobins. He never went out of doors, indeed, now, without an escort of Jacobins armed with bludgeons. An incident occurred about this time which was dexterously used by his enemies to throw ridicule on the high-priest and would-be dictator. A crazy woman named Catherine Thirt, calling herself the Mother of God, proclaimed the advent of a Messiah, and in conjunction with an ex-priest, set up a kind of free masonic society. Barrere, the dexterous trimmer, drew up a clever report on the subject, in which he hinted at Robespierre's desiring to profit by the proceedings of the fanatics without naming him. Billaud, Collot, and the members of the "Committee of General Safety," who had been attached to the old Commune, and were partisans of the Worship of Reason took offence at the cultus of the Supreme. Being. "You and Your Supreme Being," Billaud was heard to say in a stage-aside on the occasion, "are beginning to bore me." It was now a case of "aut Caesar, aut nullus," with Robespierre.

Thermidor

It now became a matter of life and death to Robespierre to overthrow the hostile members of the committees and get himself recognised as dictator. St Just tried it on behalf of his friend several times with the "Public Safety", but without effect. St. Just, by the way was probably the most sincere and enthusiastic of all followers of Robespierre. Not yet twenty-five years of age he had made a great mark on the Revolution. His large poetic eyes, his tall and dignified figure, his long dark hair, had obtained for him the nickname "of the apocalyptic." It was necessary to take action without delay. The whole of the Committee of General Security and the majority of the Committee of Public Safety were against him. The Convention therefore had to be tried, and failing the Convention an insurrection proclaimed, headed by the Jacobins and the Commune. The latter bodies were prepared some time beforehand to resort to force if necessary to the ends of their champion, and a conspiracy was actually formed, the leaders of which were St. Just, Couthon, who, together with Robespierre, constituted the so-called triumvirate, the Mayor Fleuriot, the "national agent" Payan and Dumas, the president, and Coffinhal, the vice-president of the Revolutionary Tribunal. St. Just had been recalled in great haste by Robespierre from his mission with the army of the North, and when apprised of the state of affairs he advised an immediate coup d'état. This, however, was impracticable. The Convention had to be sounded first, otherwise the pretext for rising was wanting. Accordingly early on the 26th of July (8th of Thermidor) Robespierre repaired to the Assembly and opened the sitting with along and dexterous speech, denouncing the Committees and defending himself in the name of the national sovereignty. He wound up by recommending a general "purification" all round of the Committees and of the Convention.

Robespierre sat down amid absolute silence. Not a sound or word of applause greeted his challenge. Presently, a member, Lecointre, rose and moved the printing and circulation of the harangue. This was at once vigorously resisted, but was eventually carried.

The members of the two Committees, hitherto silent now took up the challenge. They attacked Robespierre in turn. The upshot was that the decree for the printing and circulation of the discourse was virtually rescinded, being referred to the Committees for examination. Robespierre, surprised at the unwonted resistance, left the sitting discouraged, but without despairing of the situation.

In the evening he repaired to the Jacobins, when he re-read the discourse of the morning, and where it was, of course, greeted with tumultuary applause. The committees, on their side, kept together all night. Nothing during this momentous night was omitted by either party to ensure victory on the morrow. The Committees and the Mountain negotiated successfully with the Plain to bring about common action in the Assembly. Before noon the following day, July 27th (9th

Thermidor), members were to be seen encouraging each other in the corridors. The sitting was opened by St. Just. He had scarcely begun his speech, attacking the Committees, when he was interrupted and denounced by an ex-commissioner, who demanded that the veil should be withdrawn from the conspiracy. He was supported on all sides.

Billaud Varennes then spoke of "packed" meetings of Jacobins, of threats against the representatives &c. At this point of Billaud's speech the whole Convention rose and swore to defend the national sovereignty, amid the applause of the public in the galleries. All eyes were now turned towards Robespierre, who finally made a dash at the tribune. Before he could speak, however, the cry of "Down with the tyrant" resounded, throughout the hall.

Tallien, in a vigorous address, then demanded the arrest of Henriot, the commander of the reconstituted National Guard, or armed force of Paris, Billaud the arrest of other partisans of Robespierre, measures which were at once acceded to Robespierre repeatedly attempted to defend himself but his voice was always drowned with shouts of down with the tyrant and by the ringing of the President's bell. He turned to the "Plain," he turned to the public in the galleries, there was no response from either. Finally he sank down on a seat, exhausted, and foaming at the mouth.

"The blood of Danton chokes the wretch," cried a member of the Mountain.

Robespierre's arrest was demanded on all sides. His brother, Augustin Robespierre, Couthon, Lebas, and St. Just all claimed to share his fate, and were finally all given into the hands of the gendarmerie. The moment this became known at the Hotel de Ville, where the Mayor, Payan, Fleuriot and Henriot were assembled with the Commune, orders were given for the barriers to be closed, the sections assembled, the tocsin sounded, the generale beaten, and the insurrection proclaimed. The cannoneers were ordered to repair to the Place de Greve by the Hotel de Ville, and the Revolutionary Committees were hurried hither to take the oath of insurrection.

The Jacobins, who declared themselves in permanent session, formed a subordinate centre of insurrection. Henriot, who then rushed through the streets, pistol in hand, calling on the people to rise, was arrested by two deputies and brought to the Committees, but he was liberated by Coffinhal at the head of two hundred cannoneers, of which Henriot himself at once took the command, placing them in position round the Convention.

The Assembly, which had adjourned for a couple of hours, had now reassembled. It was seven o'clock. "Citizens." said the President, "Now is the time for us to die at our post." Affairs did indeed look hopeless for the Convention. Orders were almost immediately given by Henriot to fire, when, strange to say, the cannoneers, who, up to this time, had been with the insurgents, hesitated, wavered, and finally refused to comply. In the hands of those two hundred cannoneers lay the fate of France. Henriot hurried off to the Hotel de Ville. It was now the turn of the Convention to take the aggressive. The response of the sections to the call of the Commune was not altogether satisfactory. The fact is the movement of the last two days had been sudden even for Paris, and had developed out of a quarrel inside the government with which the general public were imperfectly acquainted. Though the sections assembled at nine o'clock they confined themselves to sending messages to the Commune, asking for further information.

While the assembled sections were discussing the matter in the various wards of the city delegates from the Convention arrived apprising them of the real position of affairs. They now no longer hesitated, but, arming themselves, immediately proceeded to the Tuilleries, where they were of course received with great enthusiasm. A small body, with a few pieces of artillery, having been left as a guard to the Convention the remainder then marched off to attack the head centre of the insurrection – the Hotel de Ville. The crowds which had assembled outside at the sound of the tocsin had gradually dispersed finding the sections did not arrive, and the space was now much thinned. Emissaries from the Convention proclaimed the outlawry of the insurgents, upon which all that remained went home.

The armed sections now arrived, occupied all the outlets, and set up a prolonged shout of "Long live the Convention!" The insurgents saw at once that all was lost. Robespierre shot himself, but, only succeeded in breaking his jaw. His brother threw himself from the third story. Lebas killed himself with a pistol. Couthon mangled himself with a knife. Coffinhal pitched Henriot from the window into the common sewer and managed to escape. St.Just alone awaited his fate with dignity and calmness. It was now about one-o'clock in the morning. The conspirators were conducted. First to the Committee of General Security. Robespierre lay upon a litter suffering horribly, exposed to the jeers and taunts of the bystanders, who upbraided him with all his crimes. They were afterwards taken to the prison of the Conciergerie, and brought up thence the next day before the Revolutionary tribunal, with others of their associates. They were of course, condemned, and were executed the same evening at six o'clock. Immense crowds, hooting and jeering, thronged the streets to see the tumbrils as they passed. A halt was made before the house where Robespierre had lodged. All eyes were turned on him in his "Supreme Being" blue coat and the jeers and invectives grew louder. The sullen hatred which had been growing for weeks past had suddenly found vent. At the time of his fall he probably had scarcely two or three hundred real followers in all Paris.

Instead of mitigating or abolishing the terror at the moment when the danger of invasion being past, it had no longer any solid backing in public opinion, he had chosen to exacerbate it, only too obviously for his own ambitious purposes. Thus he speedily degenerated from one of the most popular to the most hated man in all France. Robespierre was the last to ascend the scaffold. As Samson the executioner wrenched off the bloody linen which bound up his jaw a horrible yell escaped him. This was the only sign of life he had made since his arrest. The moment his head fell a roar of applause, which lasted some minutes, resounded far and wide on the evening air. Such was the celebrated revolution of "Thermidor."

The Reaction Begins

It is plain that the fall of Robespierre meant the end of the Terror, although the partisans of the system on the Committee could not see it. The Billaud Varennes, Collot D'Herbois, and Barreres thought still to carry on the proscriptions with the other methods of revolutionary government. They lost influence every day. The Terror was at once abolished, except for the "tail" of Robespierre, the members of the Commune, some of the leading Robespierrists, Jacobins, &c., who were guillotined to the number of some hundred and fifty in a few days. In the relief which even "Sans culottes" felt at being rid of the perpetual Damocles' sword, of Tinville, and of the endless rant about "virtue," "austerity," "incorruptibility" with which Robespierre and his crew had sickened everyone, they little thought that the end of the Revolution itself, in so far as it interested the working classes of France; was at hand. In truth, the reaction had begun four months before, with the execution of the party of the old Commune the Hébertists.

When a Revolution proceeds to exterminate its most enthusiastic adherents its fate is obviously sealed. Robespierre had denounced the Hebertists as Atheists and Communists, To the inventor of the "Supreme Being" and the "declaration of rights," which was foisted upon the Jacobins in opposition to Chaumette and Hebert, and according to which "the right of property is the right of every citizen to enjoy and dispose as he pleases of his goods," which provided also that "no commerce should be prohibited," and no property ever confiscated even for public purposes "without indemnity" to such a one the Hébertists were offensive without doubt.

What Robespierre desired was in short a Republic of starched, middle-class prigs, of which he himself was to be the type. The Hébertists, especially men like Chaumette and Anacharsis Clootz, whatever their faults may have been, at least desired a change better worth fighting for than this. Their instincts were Socialistic, though their ideas may have been vague, as they could scarcely fail to have been a century ago, when the "great industry" had hardly begun. As to the Terror, Robespierre substituted for the irregular methods of the Commune a systematic plan of butchery, which enabled him to rid himself conveniently of personal enemies. Still, even Robespierre, in spite of their contradicting the free Trade principles he had laid down, did not dare to suggest abolishing the maximum and other measures passed under the influence of the Commune for ensuring a possible livelihood to the working classes. This it was reserved for the Thermidorians to do.

The Committeemen had accepted the aid of the Convention in overthrowing Robespierre and his party. They soon found that the Convention was as determined to rid itself of the dictatorship of the Committees as the committees themselves had been that of Robespierre. The very next day the committees began to be attacked. The abolition of the Revolutionary Tribunal was proposed, Barrere, who spoke in its support, was taunted with having been a constitutional royalist before the 10th of August. The Convention nevertheless confined itself this time to issuing a decree of accusation against Fouquier Tinville and abolishing the law of Prairial.

The Committees themselves were next reorganised and their power curtailed. The Paris Commune never again rose after its second defeat under Robespierre. The old suspects were gradually released from prison. But the reaction did not stop at abolishing the terror. It began at once undoing all the "Sansculottic" work of the Revolution. First, the daily meetings of the sections were reduced to one in ten days. Next the allowance of twenty sous a day for indigent members was done away with. Next, the maximum was abolished. The commissioners Labon and Carrier (the author of the noyades at Nantes) were now tried. Most of the old members of. the Committees shortly after; this either resigned or were ousted, and their places were filled with Thermidorians.

Fréron, an; ex-Mountainist and now reactionist, started a paper in which he proposed that the youth of the upper and Middle-classes should arm themselves with loaded sticks to resist the Sansculottes. The suggestion was eagerly, adopted, and a new and fantastic dress was assumed as a counter-blast to the Carmagnole costume of the popular party. An open-breasted front, long hair, done up behind in tresses, called cadenettes, and low shoes, formed the costume à la victime of the "Jeunesse dorée" (gilded youth), as they were called. Every day street fights took place between them and the Jacobins. The latter, though they had undergone one of their customary purificiations after the fall of Robespierre, and had duly sent a deputation congratulating the Convention on the death of "the tyrant" found themselves daily getting into worse odour with the dominant party.

The Convention before long broke up the vast federation of clubs of which the Paris Jacobins' was the head by arbitrarily forbidding any further correspondence between the centre and the provincial branches. The Assembly, at the same time, declined to receive any further Jacobin deputations. Nevertheless the club was still the rallying point of every revolutionary influence in Paris. An attempt was made to liberate Carrier, which, although unsuccessful gave rise to a formidable disturbance, and led to the suspension of the Jacobin sittings by the Convention. The members assembled the next day notwithstanding, in defiance of the decree, but the meeting-place was attacked by the "gilded youth", and the Jacobins driven out. The Convention thereupon suppressed the club altogether. (November 12).

The Thermidorian party at first wanted a revolutionary reputation to counterbalance that of Robespierre and chose Marat, who, owing to the jealousy of the former, had not as yet received the honours of the Pantheon, which the Convention had granted after his death. But it was not long before the reputation of Marat, like everything else belonging to the Proletarian side of the Revolution, fell under the ban of the reactionary party. His busts were everywhere destroyed, and his name became the byeword has been ever since, or at least until quite recently.

The decree of expulsion agains the nobles and priests was now rescinded. The seventy-three members who had protested against the expulsion of the Girondins were released from prison and reinstated in their places in the Convention. The monument in front of the "Invalides," celebrating the victor of the Mountain over the Gironde, was destroyed. Soon after this the few remaining Girondist leaders who had come out of hiding, were received back into the Convention, thus further strengthening the great "moderate party" which had formed out of the wreckage of various parties. In January, 1795, the churches were again opened for Christian worship, though here some caution was observed, a good many restrictions on religious propagandism being still maintained. The armies were now supplied by contract instead of by requisitions on private property as heretofore. The confiscated goods of suspects and of those executed during the Terror, were restored in the first instance to themselves, in the second to their nearest relations.

The Reaction Progresses.

The reaction was daily growing in intensity. The fury of the new "White Terror" in Paris had reached other leaders than Carrier and Lebon, both of whom had been guillotined. These other leaders were our old friends Billaud Varennes, Collot D'Herbois and Barrere, together with Vadier. A demonstration in their favour, organised by the workmen's faubourgs of St. Antoine and St. Marceau, availed nothing. On 1st March (1st Germinal) they were brought before the Convention, and the proceedings lasted nine days.

Though gallantly defended by the wreck of the Mountain, they were like to be condemned, when once more the loyal Workmen's quarters made an attempt to rescue them and stormed the Convention to the cry of "Bread, the Constitution of '93, and the Liberty of the Patriots." This, too, proved abortive. Yet possibly fear of popular resentment prevented the Convention from passing a capital sentence this time. It confined itself to condemning the accused to transportation to Cayenne, where Collot took the yellow fever, drank a whole bottle of brandy, and died; and Billaud amused himself with breeding negroes and tame parrots.

The turn of Fouquier Tinville and the jurymen of the revolutionary tribunal came next. They were condemned and executed early in May. "Where are now thy batches?" mockingly exclaimed some of the crowd, as Fouquier mounted the scaffold. "Wretched canaille," replied he, "is your bread any the cheaper for not having them?" In truth, the economic situation was fearful. The abolition of the maximum and the forced currency produced a terrific crisis. The value of 5,000 francs in paper (assignats) sank to 20 francs in silver or gold. Forestalling, swindling, and extortion of every kind had a high time of it. Never before had starvation claimed so many victims as now. Death by the guillotine was succeeded by death from hunger. The crowds at the bakers' doors were worse than even before the Revolution. Bitterly did St. Antoine and St. Marceau look back on the time when., under the Commune and the Committees, they had a sufficiency and power.

The last of the popular insurrections (unless we include the abortive Babeuf conspiracy as one) took place on the 20th May (1st Prairial) of this year, 1793 (III), and was a well-organised and determined movement, but lacked leaders and staying power, and consequently fell through. The chief demands were still "Bread, the Constitution of '93, he Release of all imprisoned patriots,", &c. The faubourgs this time marched fully armed upon the Convention, which was taken by surprise, the daily recurring disturbances having hidden from it the fact that an organised insurrection was brewing. The doors were forced, and the sansculottes rushed in. At first repulsed, they returned in greater numbers. They fired at the president, Boissy D'Anglas. A deputy, – Féraud, who rushed forward to protect him, was cut down by sabres, and his head fixed on a pike. All the deputies now fled except those forming the rump of the old Mountain, to the number of about sixty, Romme (him of the calendar) now took the chair, and all the demands of the insurgents were put and carried in rapid succession.

But the wealthy "sections" had been apprised of what had happened and had meantime quietly surrounded the Tuilleries. Finally, a drilled body of Jeunesse Dorée suddenly burst in and drove out the insurgents in confusion at the point of the bayonet. The deputies re-entered. All the decrees just passed were annulled. The members of the "Mountain" were arrested as accomplices of the insurgents, and secretly conveyed away from Paris. But the "sansculottes" did not consider themselves beaten. Next day they again assembled in the outer faubourgs and proceeded to march on the Convention, this time taking their cannon with them. The inner or wealthy middle-class sections were also drawn up in arms on the Place du Carrousel in defence of the assembly. The cannon of the Faubourgs was already pointed on the Tuilleries when the Convention sent commissioners to treat with the insurgents. Their demands were pretended to be favourably received, but nothing was definitely promised. This sufficed, however, to put the "sansculottes" off their guard. Not having an energetic commune and a determined commander at their back as on the 31st of May, 1793, they retired satisfied with some vague conciliatory phrases, a course proving fatal to the insurrection which, at the opening of the day, had stood a fair chance of success, and fatal also as the event showed to the cause of the democracy.

A few days later the assassin of Féraud who had been tried and condemned to death was on his way to execution when the populace delivered him and carried him in triumph into the Faubourgs. The Convention then ordered the latter to be disarmed. The interior sections surrounded the working-class quarters the next day for the purpose of carrying out this decree. After some resistance it was effected. The Faubourgs surrendered unconditionally with their arms and cannon.

The Paris working classes were now reduced, therefore, to the condition of an unarmed mob, and for them organised insurrection was a thing of the past. Royalism became again fashionable. It was openly advocated in newspapers and in public assemblies, and even inside the Convention itself, though here it remained in a minority. Meanwhile, the "White Terror" was raging in the provinces far worse than in Paris. The South, especially, became the scene of wholesale massacres of all supposed to be friendly to revolutionary principles. Bands of returned "emigrants" and wealthy young men called "Companies of Jesus" and "Companies of the Sun" went about killing every revolutionist, or suspected revolutionist, they could find. The Jacobins had been arrested wholesale during the last few weeks. The prisons were broken into, and every "sansculotte" massacred. At Lyons 300 Jacobins were enclosed in a shed, which was then set fire to, a cordon being formed round it till they were consumed to a man. At Tarascon hundreds of victims were hurled from the top of a rock into the Rhone. This sort of thing went on for weeks without any attempt to stop it on the part of the authorities. The canting middle-class humbugs who have dilated on the "horrors of the French Revolution" and of the "mob" with so much unction, have prudently passed over the still worse horrors of the Reaction and the "respectable classes."

In Paris, encouraged by impunity, the Royalists at last attempted an insurrection against the Convention, finding that they were not likely to obtain a majority in that body. The immediate occasion of it was the conditions under which the Assembly was to be dissolved. The new Constitution which had been voted was very much on the model of that of 1791. A property qualification and indirect voting were, of course reintroduced, with two chambers, a council of 500, and a senate of 250 members, with an executive committee or Directory of five, having power to appoint six ministers. The electoral divisions: of France were re-organised in an antidemocratic sense. Now with this constitution the Royalists hoped to have obtained a majority in the next Parliament, and were grievously disappointed when the Convention enacted that two-thirds of the new body should be chosen from its own members. Hence the tears of the Royalists, and hence the insurrection of the wealthy and Royalist sections against the Convention on the 5th October, 1795 (13th of Vendemaire, III), the task of quelling which was entrusted by Barras, the generalissimo of the Convention, to a young artillery officer, Napoleon Bonaparte by name, a task the said young artillery officer duly accomplished by the aid of well-planted cannon on the evening of the same day.

The Babeuf Conspiracy and End of the French Revolution

The insurrection of Vendemiaire gave a slight check to the reaction which had, up to this time, gone on unimpeded. The majority of the Convention, much as they dreaded a return of real revolutionary government, were too much involved politically and economically in the Revolution to be able to tolerate a complete relapse to the old régime. What they desired was a plutocratic republic, in which money should take the place of privilege and a wealthy middle class succeed to the power of the old noblesse and the crown. And the new Constitution with its "council of five hundred," its "senate of ancients," its "Directorate," its property qualification, and its indirect suffrage, was admirably calculated to ensure this end. On the 26th of October the National Convention proclaimed itself dissolved, after an existence of three years and a month. One result of the events of the 5th October (13th Vendemiaire) was not unnaturally a greater toleration of the popular party, many of whom had taken up arms on the last mentioned date in defence of the Convention and the republic. The democrats established a club for purposes of political discussion at the Pantheon, which was for some time unmolested by the directory. The leader of the club was Gracchus Babeuf, who obtained the title of "tribune of the people." Though a member of the old Commune he had not hitherto played any important part in the Revolution.

The society at the Pantheon grew daily in numbers, and with it grew the influence of Babeuf. The members at length ventured to repair to their meeting-place in arms, and whispers of a projected insurrection soon made themselves heard. The Directory thereupon became alarmed, and on the 26th of February, 1796 (8th Ventose, IV.), peremptorily closed the Pantheon and forbade any further meetings of the club. The followers of Babeuf, among whom were the remnant of the old Commune and Committees, and of course all the old Jacobins, then resorted to direct -conspiracy and managed to win over the "legion of police," but here again they were outwitted by the Directory, which immediately disarmed and disbanded this body. The Babeuvists (as they were called) now assembled secretly in a place they named the "Temple of Reason," and concerted measures for an organised insurrection and attack on the governing bodies. They succeeded in rallying in a short time most of the revolutionary elements of France.

It was agreed to form a new Convention, of which the nucleus was to be such remnant of the old Mountain as death and proscription had left Armed. Bands were suddenly to march from several points concentrically upon the Directory and councils. The Baboevists believed themselves sure of the military stationed at the Camp of Grenelle, and an officer named Grisel was in their confidence. Everything was arranged up to the night of the projected movement. Two placards were about to be posted up, one bearing the words "Constitution of 1793, Liberty,

Equality, and general happiness." the other the motto, "Those who usurp supreme power ought to be put to death by freemen," and the signal was agree upon for action when, the chiefs were suddenly surprised and arrested in their council chamber (May 10th They had been betrayed by Grisel. Babeuf while in prison, wrote to the directors suggesting a compromise. He was nevertheless with the other leaders sent before the new high court of Vendome.

On the 7th of September following, while they were still awaiting their trial, their followers, to the number of some hundreds, made an armed attack on the Luxembourg, the palace of the directors, but were repulsed by the guards placed there for its defence. They then proceeded to the camp Grenelle, in the hope of raising the military, in which they were again unsuccessful, being met by a determined resistance. A sharp skirmish followed, ending in the complete rout of the insurgents, who left a large number of dead on the field. This was the last attempt of the democracy to recover its position.

Almost all the leaders and organisers of the Babeuf movement were executed by the sentence of military commissions, and numbers of other persons were imprisoned and exiled. Babeuf himself, and Darthé, the late secretary of Lebon, after acquitting themselves during their trial in a manly manner, fully avowing their principles, stabbed themselves to death with daggers on hearing their sentence. The objects of Babeuf and his followers were definitely and consciously communistic, which cannot be said of any other of the revolutionary parties. Babeuf himself (who, by the side of Marat, Chaumette, Clootz and Pache, may be regarded as one of the noblest and most disinterested of all the leaders of the time) if, in his theoretical scheme, he was the first of the utopian Socialists, also forestalled in his notion of the necessity of taking possession of the political power one of the foremost principles of the modern Socialist movement.

With the final extinction of the party of Babeuf in September, 1796, after which our French democracy never again rallied, the French Revolution, as a distinct event in history, may be considered to come to an end. From the meeting of the States General in May, 1789, to the date just mentioned, was only a little more than seven yeas, but what an experience France and Europe had passed through. Since Camille Desmoulins delivered his famous harangue in the Palais Royal Gardens on that July day in '89, when revolutionary ardour seemed so single in its purpose – so young and unsophisticated – how many parties had been consumed, how many enthusiasms had been burnt out!

With the forlorn attempt of the Babeuvists on Grenelle revolutionary fervour gasped its last breath. The Bourgeois had conquered; the day of the Proletarian was not yet, in spite of his temporary accession to power during the great revolutionary years.

The events succeeding the collapse of the Babeuf movement may be signalised in a few sentences. The populace of Paris and the other large cities gradually settled down into a private life of toil and hardship; and an indifference to public affairs. The wealthy classes plunged into every form of dissipation and extravagance. The new middle-class republic became apparently every day more consolidated. It flourished at home under the director Barras and his colleagues, of whom Carnot was one, and abroad under its new general, Bonaparte. Conquest again followed conquest. New republics, on the model of the French, sprang up like mushrooms in Holland, Liguria, Lombardy, Sardinia, Switzerland, etc. The fresh elections in May, 1797, nevertheless yielded a royalist majority in the Councils, the upshot of which was that Barras and the majority of the directors by the following September, when things came to a crisis, had to call in the aid of the army under General Augereau to overawe the legislature. This succeeded, and a large number of members including some "rats" of the old Dantonist party were exiled on the ground of royalist intrigue to overthrow the republic. Carnot and Barthelemy were driven from the Directory, The latter now became practically a dictatorship, with Barras as head dictator.

Most of the powers, tired of prosecuting an adverse war, were glad to make terms of peace. England soon became the only belligerent remaining. But the Directory, without money, and having only the armies to fall, back upon, could not afford to bring about a complete cessation of hostilities. Bonaparte, after having subdued the Continent, about this time returned to Paris, the most popular man in France. Barras, feeling his presence dangerous at home, invited him at once to undertake the task of subduing the British power. He readily acceded, and the brilliant Egyptian campaign entered upon with a view to India, was the result. The elections of 1798 which were, unlike those of the previous year, too radical to please the directory, were annulled, but those of the following year, 1799, produced the same result.

Meanwhile a new coalition had been formed, one of the principal factors of which was Russia. The unpopular directory could now no longer hold out against public opinion. Negotiations between the various parties were entered into without issue, and the government at home was in great confusion when Bonaparte suddenly appeared on the scene, having left his oriental army in the hands of General Kléber. A conspiracy was at once formed, led by the old constitutionalist Sièyes, to place dictatorial authority in the hands of the successful general. The Senate, seduced by the report of a pretended Jacobin insurrection in the departments, which was to shortly reach the capital, consented to decree the removal of both houses of legislature to the palace of St. Cloud, near Paris, and to placing Bonaparte at the head of the military forces.

This was the 9th November, 1799 (18th Brumaire, VII). The following day the legislature removed to St. Cloud. The "Council of Ancients" met in the "Gallery of Mars," one of the apartments of the old Palace, and the council of five hundred in the "Orangery." The "Council of Five Hundred" unanimously swore to the existing constitution, refusing to ratify the powers given by the other body. Bonaparte was driven away with cries of "down with the tyrant," &c. His brother, Lucien Bonaparte, who was president, finding nothing was to be done, came out and harangued the troops, stating that the assembly was being intimidated by a minority of the members with drawn daggers. Bonaparte, thus fortified then gave orders for the "orangery" to be cleared by the military, which was immediately effected. Thus was the Consulate founded. From this, to the consecration as Emperor in 1804 was but a step.

The National Property.

The course of the Revolution cannot be properly estimated without taking into consideration the results of the confiscation of the property of the nobility and clergy, and afterwards of that of the guillotined. In the directoral constitution of 1795 (III.) we read, Article 374: "The French nation proclaims, as guarantee of public faith, that after an adjudication legally consummated, of the national goods, whatever may be its origin, the legitimate acquirer thereof cannot be dispossessed." The same clause, but slightly modified, is introduced into the Consular Constitution of 1800 (VIII.), and the Imperial Constitution of 1804 (XII). There is more than meets the eye in these articles. They are the issue and sanction of a series of transactions which established a wealthy plutocracy on the ruins of the old feudal aristocracy of France.

The first property to be sold was that of the church. This, which in a sense may be considered as having been held in trust for the poor, was primarily disposed of, not to benefit them, but to reduce the public debt. The sales began in 1789, and the period of greatest activity was from August 1790 to January 1791. French companies, English companies, Dutch companies disputed for the spoil, only a comparatively few lots falling to the share of the peasantry. The sales were the more easily effected inasmuch as only a small percentage of the purchase-money had to be paid down. When the time came for the second instalment the money for payment was, naturally, considering the vast extent of the purchases, in many cases not available. This led many of the speculators to favour the Revolution, and all of them to urge on the foreign war, both of which would serve as an excuse for postponement. War was accordingly proclaimed in April, 1792, and the following August the throne was overturned. After the latter event it was decided that the lands and property of the emigrant aristocrats should not be sold haphazard and en masse like the ecclesiastical property, but should be duly apportioned into small lots, which the small cultivator might hire or purchase on easy terms.

This concession on the part of the middle classes was, however, simply the result of fear of imminent foreign invasion. No sooner had the armies of Dumouriez driven the enemy back than a new assembly, the Convention, announced that the partition of the public land; must be indefinitely postponed. During the winter '92-3 the movable effects of the "emigrants" came into the possession of speculators and jobbers by means of sham sales. So flagrant was the abuse that the Convention had to step in, but without much effect. After the fall of the Girondins the partition of the communal lands was again definitely ordered. The second grand campaign now intervened, arid France was for the moment converted into one vast camp. Exceptional measures were the order of things all round, and few transfers were effected. But this did not prevent the confiscation both of lands and movables of the nobles and suspects going on at a greater pace than ever. The various agents of the Government in the departments made fortunes by clever manoeuvring. Two-thirds of the houses in Paris were now national property. The Convention decreed that "goods" to the value of one milliard should be reserved for the citizen soldiers returned from the wars. This milliard, we need scarcely say, remained a promise to the end of the chapter.

The Committee of Public Safety, early '94, ordered the sale of the confiscated lands to be proceeded with, but while recommending that the principle of partition should be adopted, did not insist upon it, the net result of the a new sales being that large tracts of public land went into the possession of a new class of thieves; to wit, the victuallers of the armies.

Robespierre, through his agent St. Just, now got a decree passed that indigent patriots should be indemnified out of the goods of the "enemies of the Revolution," but this decree was merely procured to maintain his popularity with the people, and was never so much as attempted to be put into execution.

The 9th of Thermidor arrived without the working classes of the towns having touched any of the "goods" of the emigrants, the clergy, or the suspects, while the peasantry had to be satisfied with here and there a few crumbs in the shape of the partition of communal lands. Barrere had said that they had coined money on the Place de la Revolution, but the working classes cannot be accused of having shared in this ill-gotten gain.

After the revolution of Thermidor the traffic in the "national property" proceeded more unblushingly than ever. As soon as the maximum was abolished, however, the plutocracy found it more to their interest to hocus the currency than to purchase lands at however reduced a money value. By procuring a practically unlimited issue of paper they succeeded in reducing the value of the assignats to next to nothing. The forestalling of the necessaries of life, which was the immediate cause of the various insurrections after Thermidor up to that of Baboeuf was also a stupendous source of gain. The reopening of the Bourse, the repudiation of the hypothec of the assignats on the confiscated lands, the latter a piece of thieving of the most impudent character, followed in the natural course of things. Lotteries were instituted, the prizes of which were the "national property." One deputy even had the impudence to propose to take back the lands already distributed amongst the peasantry. This was thought to be too risky, however. Meanwhile the victories of the armies under Bonaparte opened fresh fields and pastures new for every form of swindling by means of provisioning "contracts." Verily a cessation of the war would have been a grievous thing for the rising plutocracy of France. Under the directory the exploiters flung themselves anew upon the as yet undistributed territories. Everything was now in their own hands. No stone was left unturned to diminish for the nonce the market value of this property. The which was paid in depreciated paper taken at the nominal value was in most cases simply farcical.

But all means of robbing were not yet exhausted. The army contractors refused to be paid any longer in assignats, but insisted on large sums being placed to their credit in the books of the national debt, thus saddling themselves in perpetuity on the French people. Deputies,

Government, agents, generals, contractors, engaged in a mad scramble which could make the most out of the situation. The masses of France had but two purposes in their eyes – to labour at home and at starvation wages, insufficient to support life for any but the strongest, and to serve as food for powder abroad. The vast territorial estates of the feudal aristocracy, and the house property of the towns, thus passed into the hands of another and a meaner set of lords. The new middle class of France was consolidated economically and politically. Verily the French Revolution was a success – for them. And now having reached the summit of their ambition it only remained to kick over the ladder which had helped them up. The hearth, the throne, and the altar must be re-established on a new basis; we must have done with revolution and all its ways, said they. Revolution must be henceforth a thing accursed, But a republic, however, safeguarded against the intrusion of the "common people," seemed to many an insufficient guarantee under the existing circumstances for the newly created "order." A military dictator, who knew bow to smother insurrections in the birth, he was the man for the situation, and his name was – Napoleon Bonaparte.

Conclusion

The French Revolution closes in a final and definite manner an epoch in the world's history. The middle ages proper, it is true, came to an end with the 16th century. But they left a kind of afterglow behind them in the shape of the centralised and quasi-absolutist princedoms and monarchies which prevailed during the 17th and 18th centuries; in the continuance in rural districts and the smaller towns of the old methods of industry but slightly, if at all, modified; in the perpetuation unabated for over a century at least of mediaeval and renaissance superstitions and habits of thought; but slightly if at all modified in short in the survival of most of the external forms of the old-world civilisation, decayed as in a St. Martin's summer. The conversion of the feudal hierarchies into centralised monarchies but imperfectly freed the middle classes; the combined or workshop system of production had not in any marked or violent manner revolutionised industry ; the learning of the renaissance had, to a large extent, merely given a quasi-scientific and systematic shape of to old habits of thought.

The leading political, moral and social changes leading on to modern times were of changes course going on all the while, and were observable to the truly observant, but were not precisely a "run and read" character.

The French Revolution definitely closes this epoch. It does even more. It constitutes the dividing line between a world to-day and all past ages whatever. The Revolution was scarcely over when the electric telegraph appeared on the scene. At the same time the idea of the steam engine was brewing in the heads of the ingenious, and the closing years of the century saw the first of the new industrial machines established in the factories of the north of England. New stage-coach roads, canals, and then "improvements" sprang up in all directions. A couple of decades or so more and the great industry was to start of human production the metamorphosis of human production and distribution, yet another, and the railway was to begin the transformation of the face of nature and the externals of human life in other directions. In short, from the French Revolution we advance straight by leaps and bounds to the modem world.

The city of Paris well typifies the progress. One hundred years ago, in 1789 it was (unlike London, which in its mediaeval form was destroyed by the fire of 1666) to all intents and purposes a mediaeval city, substantially the Paris of Victor Hugo's Notre Dame, a city of feudal fortresses high-walled enclosures, crooked narrow, unpaved streets.

The Committee of Public Safety in 1793 began alterations. Partly with a view of giving employment to distressed workmen. The changes went on gradually till, in 1859, Haussmann, under Napoleon III., totally destroyed what remained of old Paris, and laid out the city in the form we see it to-day – a city which would be as foreign to Danton, Robespierre or Marat as San Francisco itself. The Paris of centuries perished in little more than fifty years. What is true of

Paris is true of Europe – of the whole of existing civilisation. The Europe of 1789 was in the main the Europe of the late middle ages – of the Renaissance – but in the last stage of decay. It had been practically dead for over two centuries, and like Edgar Poe's mesmerised dead man it fell to pieces with a sudden convulsive awaking. No restoration could bring it together again. The new world of our time had meantime grown up with its science, its inventions, its intense self-consciousness, and placed insurmountable barrier, between us and our naive and simple-minded ancestors. In politics the reign of the bourgeoisie with its oppression resting on cunning and hypocrisy has long shut out the possibility of an enduring reaction to the coarse and more direct methods of feudal domination.

There are several points worthy of notice, afforded by the course of the French Revolution. One feature of the period, already alluded to, its perpetual reference to classical models, and its somewhat mechanical attempt to make history repeat itself, to reproduce the republics of ancient Greece and Rome in 18th century France, can never be left out of sight. Every man's head was full of Plutarch's lives. All men, however little else they knew, seem to have had at least a superficial school-boy smattering of Roman history. Almost every speech and every newspaper article of the time bristles with references to Coriolanus, Cato, Cicero, Brutus, Caesar, &c. In fact Roman history was to the French Revolution very much what the Jewish annals, contained in the Bible, were to the English rebellion under Charles I. We, or rather modern science and historical criticism, have changed all that. We no longer look to the past as a model for the society of the present or the future. The doctrine of evolution has taught us that human society, like everything else, is a growth, and that though corresponding and analogous phases certainly do recur in history, we can yet never argue back from one period to another, as though there had been no intervening development, and as though the economical, intellectual and political conditions were substantially the same, or might be made the same.

Another point the Revolution teaches us is the effective power of minorities. The Terror itself (whatever view we may take as to its justifiability), it cannot be denied, was kept up for nearly two years by a comparatively small but energetic minority in all the towns of France. Outside this minority (the Jacobins) there was a floating mass of inert sympathy with the objects of Sansculottism, and a belief in the necessity of drastic measures in view of the situation. Beyond this, again, was the vast mass of inert stupidity and indifference which was effectually cowed. The active enemies of the Revolution were, of course, reduced to silence. It is significant to notice that most of the great crises were connected with affairs on the frontiers. The 10th of August and the September massacres were the response to Brunswick's manifesto, and the march of the enemy on the capital respectively. The 31st of May was directly brought about by the invasion of the new coalition and the disorganisation of Dumouriez's armies, consequent on his defection. Finally, the 9th Thermidor and the abolition of the "Terror," followed on the disappearance of the last trace of danger from the foreigner by the victories of the army of the north. The extraordinary enthusiasm which we find, the reckless readiness of all alike to inflict and to suffer death might lead us to suppose the men of the time to have been a race of born heroes, or monsters, or both. The average of them were neither the one nor the other. They were the products of social forces beyond their control. The feeling of the all-importance of the public interest carried all before it. Prior to the revolution they were probably either more courageous nor more truculent than ourselves. The same courage and the same truculency might manifest itself in any man of character under like circumstances. Even Robespierre was, as Carlyle suggests, probably neither better nor worse than other attorneys to start with. But in his case ambition ultimately assumed the mastery over his whole personality. This was partly owing to the fact that he was undeniably a man without a vice (in the ordinary sense of the word). Now only very exceptional men can afford to be without the ordinary vices of mankind and Robespierre was certainly not one of these men. With his ascetic Rousseauite notions of republican austerity he had suppressed his natural appetites, the consequence being that all the morbid elements in his character, having no other outlet, ran into the channel of self-idolatry and morbid ambition. The first condition of a well regulated man is to know how to properly distribute the quantum of vice with which a bountiful nature has endowed him. A false morality teaches him to suppress it. But this he can seldom do, and if he succeeds, it is at the expense of all or much that is distinctive in his character. In tearing off the coating of vice, he tears off his skin with it. The usual case, however, is that the vice is not got rid of, but only forced into some out-of-the way channel. And whenever vice is concentrated it is bad. When all the vice of a character is focussed on any single one of the natural appetites, a man becomes a sot, a satyr, a glutton, a confirmed gambler, &c. Robespierre sat upon all these valves. He and his ascetic band poured scorn on the Hébertists and the Dantonists alike for the "looseness" of their lives. But having closed up all the ordinary exits his vice came out none the less concentrated, but in the form of a truculent, remorseless ambition, of a quite peculiar kind.

The rank and file of the actors in the revolution it is difficult, for the reasons before stated, to characterise by any of the ordinary ethical standards. The best of them did things we cannot always approve while sitting comfortably in our chairs, the worst of them showed much genuine and disinterested devotion to the cause of the people. Were we called upon to name the five men whose aims were probably the purest we would mention Marat, Chaumette, Clootz, Fache, and Babeuf. Danton, apart from the disputed question of his bribery, was a mere politician, who only interested himself in social questions, when at all, in so far as they immediately affected the political situation.

The issue of the French Revolution was, as we have seen, the modern world of great capital and free trade, as opposed to the old world of land and privilege. In France, the political side of the great change was most prominent; in Germany, the philosophical and literary; in England, the industrial. While French politicians were engaged in establishing the republic, German thinkers were engaged in founding 19th century thought, and English inventors in establishing new modes of locomotion and production. But while the mediaeval organisation of society held together for centuries, the modern is already showing signs of approaching dissolution. Why is this? We answer, because the, latter contained, from the first, in its very nature, the seeds of dissolution. The capitalistic, system of necessity feeds upon, itself. Competition, which is the breath of its life, of necessity also destroys that life. It may be that the "opening up" of Africa and other as yet unexploited territories will give the system a further lease of existence, lasting some decades, but the end cannot in any case be a long by-and-bye.

THE END

Made in the USA
Middletown, DE
16 July 2022

69539481R00046